DESIGNING DEFENSE FOR A NEW WORLD ORDER

THE MILITARY BUDGET IN 1992 AND BEYOND

DESIGNING DEFENSE FOR A NEW WORLD ORDER

THE MILITARY BUDGET IN 1992 AND BEYOND

EARL C. RAVENAL

CATO INSTITUTE
Washington D.C.

Library of Congress Cataloging-in-Publication Data

Ravenal, Earl C.
  Designing defense for a new world order : the military budget in 1992
and beyond / by Earl C. Ravenal.
      p. cm.
    Includes bibliographical references.
    ISBN 0–932790–86–0 : $9.95.
    United States—Military policy.   2. United States—Armed
Forces—Appropriations and expenditures.   3. United States—Foreign
relations—1989–   I. Title.
UA23.R193   1991   91–27226
355'.0335'73—dc20   CIP

Cover design by Colin Moore.

Printed in the United States of America.

CATO INSTITUTE
224 Second Street, S.E.
Washington, D.C. 20003

Contents

THE BUSH 1992 DEFENSE PROGRAM:
"TWO TIMES THREE-QUARTER WARS"   1

THE SITUATION OF THE UNITED STATES IN THE WORLD   7

GEOPOLITICAL LESSONS FROM THE PERSIAN GULF   11

THE FUTURE SHAPE OF THE INTERNATIONAL SYSTEM   21

IMPLICATIONS FOR SECURITY   31

THE SO-WHAT FACTOR   37

THE EXAMPLE OF THE PERSIAN GULF   43

PRINCIPLES FOR NATIONAL SECURITY   59

THE DEFENSE DEBATE   73

FORCE AND BUDGETARY PLANNING   77

EPILOGUE: A NATION AMONG NATIONS   81

The Bush 1992 Defense Program: "Two Times Three-Quarter Wars"

Global intervention—adopting every country's threats—is the strategic premise of the Bush administration's post–Persian Gulf defense program for fiscal year 1992.[1] That defense program was dropped rather inconspicuously into the slipstream of the Persian Gulf War.[2] The Bush administration's 1992 defense program is not just a bunch of numbers. It incorporates two main ideas:

1. It continues to take savings, measured against the "original" defense program enunciated by the incoming Bush administration on April 25, 1989, accomplishing a projected "peace dividend," through FY 1996, of $397 billion.
2. It transcends the cold-war "bipolar" military orientation, committed to containing Soviet and other communist expansion; yet it harbors a substitute global interventionist design, as well as a residual commitment to present allies.

Defense budgets express, and must be measured against, some larger concept of national security and, beyond that, some foreign policy and view of the world. Thus, this defense budget represents the Bush administration's projection of the post–Persian Gulf world and the political-military role of the United States in that world. It incorporates an inchoate "Bush Doctrine"—which seems to be that the United States must protect a scheme of world order, a sort of combined "unipolar world" and regime of collective security, and

[1]Secretary of Defense Dick Cheney, *Annual Report to the President and the Congress* for fiscal year 1992 (Washington: U.S. Government Printing Office, 1991). It is dated January 1991 but was delivered to the Senate Armed Services Committee on February 21, 1991.

[2]The defense budget request did not incorporate the incremental cost of the war itself, which is the subject of a supplemental request. Thus, my study also does not include the supplemental war costs in the defense budget figures for 1991 and 1992, but it does cite those costs in the appropriate discussions.

1

that, specifically, the United States has extensive interests in various regions that may require military intervention.

It is only fair to observe that the Bush administration is planning a significant reduction of general purpose forces (measured by the decrease from 21 land divisions at the start of 1990 to 17 land divisions at the end of 1992, (and beyond that, to 15 land divisions in 1995). More important, in terms of this administration's defensive purposes, is a restructuring of the regional attributions of forces (which must be inferred from various indications in the secretary of defense's 1992 "posture statement"). In my analysis, ground forces (and along with them, roughly proportional segments of tactical air and surface naval forces) primarily allocated to a European contingency decrease from the FY 1990 defense program's 11⅔ divisions to the FY 1992 program's 7⅓ divisions. Correspondingly, ground forces dedicated to an "other regional" (other than Europe or East Asia) contingency increase from the 5⅔ divisions of FY 1990 to the 6⅔ divisions of FY 1992. (Ground forces identified for East Asia decrease moderately from 3⅔ to 3 divisions.)

What this reflects is the arrival of the post–cold war world, or the implementation of Bush's "new world order." This is more than a mere slogan; it has—at least now—a tangible, operational concomitant in our force structure and defense budget. In effect (without quite putting it in such terms), Bush is moving from Reagan's "1½ (ample) wars"—which followed Carter's "1½ (NATO-weighted) wars" and, before that, Nixon's "1½ wars," which radically shifted from Johnson's and Kennedy's "2½ wars"—to a new force-sizing concept that could be called "two times three-quarter wars," since the possible second war (such as that in the Persian Gulf) might be as large as the (now scaled-down) European war.

One thing is clear about the new world order: it is not self-enforcing. It depends on American power. To address the possible simultaneity of conflicts, the United States must have fairly large and redundant forces. To confront a variety of possible adversaries, it will need a range of modern, capable forces, in turn requiring advanced technology and considerable research and development. To cope with initial defense (not just counterattack), it must have ready, deployed or deployable, units and forward logistical bases and pre-positioned equipment on land and sea; and for this, it needs allies that will have to be favored in various military, diplomatic, and economic ways.

2

Collective security does not mean net burden shifting. Rather, it creates liabilities (commitments to allies, military and economic assistance) at the same rate as assets (bases, overflight, cooperative forces, some financial contributions). In a sense, the United States is acquiring every nation's enemies.

True, without a permanent adversary in the form of the Soviet Union, we might decline some invitations to conflict. But Bush's 1992 defense program is a prescription that is still expensive and potentially escalatory. It is expressive not so much of a state of affairs "beyond containment" as of a globalization of containment. It universalizes threats, and it hopes to collectivize the military response, always under American direction. America remains the world's policeman—even more so, since it undertakes to protect against a full spectrum of challenges in any and all regions.

Some important details of America's geopolitical situation hinge on the regional alignment that will follow the gulf war. Yet the war illustrates, rather than alters, a more general state of affairs that was already shaping up in the wake of the cold war, before Saddam Hussein's invasion of Kuwait on August 2, 1990. The events in the Persian Gulf must be read as evidence of the unfolding future of the international system and particularly as an object lesson in the propriety of American military intervention in the impending new system.

All the more reason, then, to step back from the pressing and poignant events of the present and gain some perspective—even to the point of abstraction—on the situation of the United States in the world. We should be looking, not for specific guidance on particular deployments or individual weapons systems, but for general principles of orientation and organization that are appropriate to the emerging state of affairs. And we should be trying to discern, not particular threats—specific things against which the United States must prepare, in detail, to defend—but rather the kind of world, with its characteristic disturbances, that we will be facing as far out as the horizon of 15 to 30 years, so that we may form some judgment about whether such disturbances will constitute integral threats to American society.

Defense programs—not just the budget dollars, but the number and quality of forces, the kinds of major weapons systems, the operational doctrines, and the number of military pesonnel—are mainly driven (despite the alleged influence of the military-industrial complex or certain cognitive or ideological obsessions) by the large-scale factors of the nation's situation in the world (roughly, "geopolitics") played against the constraints that arise from the domestic political (including constitutional)-economic-social system (roughly, "political economy"). And the nation's large-scale foreign policy and military strategy choices are (in a quasi-rational process not always clearly recognized as such) the product of a kind of cost-benefit weighing, in which the nation's sacrifices are matched to the prospective results, in its welfare and security, that might be brought about by intervening and preparing to intervene with military force in various circumstances in the world.

From that perspective, it appears that the United States is at a significant historical juncture—a crossroads in its own foreign policy orientation and in the course of the international system (which a great nation, such as the United States, still influences, though markedly less than it might have 45 years ago, after another great conflict of global proportions). The United States has two choices. It can further the system that I call collective security (not individual peacekeeping episodes but an entire system devoted to mobilizing the "preponderance" of nations, as Woodrow Wilson put it, against any transgression—more or less what President Bush has been calling a new world order). Or it can acquiesce in the system (some would call it the nonsystem) of "general unalignment," characterized by the emergence of perhaps a dozen and a half autonomous centers of political-military initiative in various regions of the world, the extensive fragmentation and "regionalization" of power, and the dissolution of military alliances and many other political and even economic groupings of nations. In my view, despite the apparent success of President Bush in mobilizing an international coalition to repel and punish Iraqi aggression in the gulf, the odds, in the aftermath of the gulf episode, favor a lapse into the system of general unalignment.

From the standpoint of American national security, the system of general unalignment will be characterized primarily by the absence of an important, coordinated political-military threat to the integrity and status of the United States and American society (unless, of course, we go out to meet or anticipate presumed threats, as we did in the Persian Gulf). In other words, in the wake of the

4

half-century of cold war and in the impending system of general unalignment, disturbances in the world (what people call "threats") will be legion, but they will be diffuse, even elusive, and no power, no constellation of circumstances, will be able to impair the essential security of the United States. This fortunate state of affairs—for the United States, not necessarily for other countries—if we understand it and grasp it, will prevail out to the horizon of the future.

The nation's purposes in the world can be read more accurately and more "operationally" in its tangible possession and disposition of forces than in its rhetorical formulations—those authoritative policy pronouncements by "leaders" that are taken by most observers to constitute the nation's foreign policy (and are debated mostly in terms of how attractive and worthy are the enunciated goals). It is the force structure, and the implicit "missions" built into the number, nature, and disposition of the forces, that tell us what a country's national strategy and foreign policy really are.

In these operational terms, the Bush defense program is all dressed up and looking for a place to go (and, not accidentally, has found such a place in the Persian Gulf). Two years after the official repudiation of containment, the defense program is a containment program, but with two notable variations: (1) it offers universal containment, of any disturbance, not just a threat by a principal adversary; and (2) it invokes collective enforcement, by an entire international community or an ad hoc coalition, rather than by one of two opposing military alliances. This universal and collective containment still embodies the grand "paradigm" of strategic dispositions that guided American defense policy throughout the half-century of the cold war: deterrence (now emphasizing exemplary punishment) and forward defense (now attempting to resuscitate our alliance systems by broadening them, turning them to a more comprehensive and diffuse objective). This, apparently, is the Bush administration's way of adjusting American foreign and military policy to address a new array of diverse threats from multiple sources, instead of the one-dimensional military threat from the citadel of the Soviet Union. There is a diversification of missions, and a scaled-down version of the cold war force structure is being used residually for lesser regional interventions.

In its burden on American society, the tangible difference between a defense program trimmed only marginally from the cold war and an alternative, radically reduced response to a diminished and diffused threat is extensive. Just a few seasons ago, people were calling that difference the peace dividend. Though the Bush administration has realized a fair fraction of that dividend, in terms of reductions from its original defense projections when it came into office, the further difference, over the next five years, that a noninterventionist alternative could make is $305 billion. That difference represents the commitment of the Bush administration to its misapprehension of the world.

The Situation of the United States in the World

Ultimately then, a defense budget represents a view of the world and of the place and role of a nation in that world. It is on those broadest grounds that four questions must be asked when considering the Bush defense program.

1. Does the view of the world conform to reality?
2. Does the chosen role of the United States respond to necessity?
3. Do the proposed strategy and its implementation—in force structure, major weapons systems, and budget dollars—appropriately support that role, and is that support consistent with the domestic resources of fiscal means and public approval?
4. Finally, if one challenges the program on the foregoing grounds, is there an alternative vision, and are there alternative means?

A defense program, embodying a nation's protection against external attack, must be the result of two sets of factors: (1) a nation's situation in the world (call this geopolitics) and (2) the resources a nation will spare for the security function and the mandate a society gives to its government to protect certain values against external attack or pressure (call these political economy). Roughly, the latter determines what a government is "paid" to defend; the former, what it defends against.

To grasp the first set of geopolitical factors, we must draw some conclusions about where the "international system" is going. The international system consists of the political-military relationships among the world's essential players (still largely nation-states)—to paraphrase Stanley Hoffmann: what nations can do to each other and what nations want to do to each other.[3] Thus, a nation's situation in this system consists, on the one hand, of its own power

---

[3]As well as, of course, "what are the units in potential conflict." See Stanley Hoffmann, "International Systems and International Law," *World Politics* 14 (1961).

resources—its population, wealth, military assets and momentum, technological and industrial potential, and a host of more subtle factors. On the other hand, it consists of the "shape" of the international system and some items of political geography. The shape of the system refers to how power is configured (who has the power and how much) in the world and the nation's immediate and somewhat larger region, how power is regulated or restrained, and what modes of external behavior are built into the decisionmaking process of each important state in the system. The items of political geography refer to a country's territorial size and its distance from potential enemies and friends, its access to strategic points and strategic commodities, its vulnerability to external harm, its natural defensive barriers, and its lines of communication to its peripheries and other global points. Conclusions about the defensive feasibility and the defensive requirements of a country must be drawn from a projection of such factors into the working future.

The other set of factors, involved in political economy—a government's construction of its proper objectives and its political mandate—can become especially controversial, because it involves those values that a state considers worth defending and, if need be, imposing by force on other states in the world. The list of such possible objects of foreign policy includes two that are particularly disputed at this moment.

One of these is the propagation, beyond our own borders, of our political values—often conceived of as human rights and democracy. The other is stability, or order—again, not in our immediate political precincts, but in other regions, and, in general, throughout the world; this is sometimes called a "milieu goal." The pursuit of those values as objects of our foreign policy has far more expansive consequences, in terms of danger and expense, than the attempt to perfect those values for and within our own society and immediate area.

It can be argued that America, after the cold war, is in a peculiarly enviable position. No other country or organized group in the world can inflict (with any plausible motive or with any serious impunity, and, therefore, with any reckonable likelihood) aggravated harm on the United States. Thus, the United States is virtually immune from harm as long as (and these are the essential conditions) (1) we do not destroy ourselves from within by governmental ineptness

8

or governmental intrusion into the workings of economy and society, and (2) our government does not distort its political mandate and project force into other parts of the world that are not amenable to that projection.

The situation of the United States in the world a short time after the termination of the cold war is rather like that of the early 1920s (but unlike that of the late 1940s) in one sense: we are many years away from the emergence of a new hostile constellation of power. And, unlike the situation of both the 1920s and the 1940s, the international system may not, for a very long time, take a structural shape that could be construed as directly threatening to the United States.

The international system is changing in the explicit sense that the parameters of the system are shifting. This is not just the trendy truism of "multipolarity" (so common now in the policy-intellectual community that, like "'plastics" in the 1960s movie *The Graduate*, it is caricatured by political cartoonists). The international system is changing in a way that will go far beyond the relatively manageable, controlled balance of power that is envisaged, and tentatively welcomed, by pundits and policy practitioners alike in the United States. They welcome it precisely because they anticipate that the United States, in the aftermath of what they conceive to be the bipolarity of the cold war, will continue to control the behavior of other countries in the world through active force, threat of force, diplomatic pressure, and manipulation and application of America's various other assets, including what Joseph Nye, in his "counter-declinism" thesis, calls "soft power."[4]

But the world already, two decades ago, entered a multipolar version of its cold war structure; this could be called the Nixon-Kissinger phase. Now, it is transcending that interim, ultimately unstable phase—unstable mostly because its principal assigned actors (a constitutionally inhibited United States, an inherently warped and debilitated Soviet Union, a ponderous and unbalanced China, a diplomatically unadventurous and critically limited Japan, and a Europe of continuingly divided second-rank powers) would not play the roles requisite to maintaining a multipolar balance-of-power system. And so, the international system is moving to an

[4]Joseph S. Nye, Jr., "Soft Power," *Foreign Policy* 80 (Fall 1990): 153–71.

even more diffused state, "beyond the balance of power," that I call general unalignment.

That is the international system that the United States faces for the midrange future of, say, 15 to 30 years (the time frame for which we ought to be designing our large-scale foreign policy orientations and national strategic attitudes). Most significant for the United States, there will be no Soviet or other major threat. A state of peace will exist in Europe, but there will not necessarily be stability, particularly within Eastern Europe. In fact, instability will characterize most parts of the international system—obviously the Middle East. The present, putative multipolar balance of power will further unravel to the point where general unalignment will establish itself. This system will be marked by the rise of regional "hegemones"[5] or at least regionally contested situations that tend to exclude or discourage extraregional intervention. Also, contrary to present perception, this situation will encourage less than expected regional integration, at least on the political level, even in Europe. An increase of nuclear proliferation will be both a cause and a result of the tendency toward fragmentation and regionalization of power. This impending situation will also bring about the irrelevance of present alliance systems, including NATO. And the entire international system will be continuously unsettled by disturbances, mostly nonstrategic, such as resource denials, restrictions of trade, environmental damage, population pressures, excessive migration, narcotics, and fanatic terrorism. Yet, even though most parts of the international system may be unstable, the system as a whole may well be "metastable," since dangerous advantages will not thereby accrue to any of the great powers or erstwhile "superpowers." Thus, even other-regional conflicts of some magnitude need not directly threaten, or even indirectly implicate, the United States.

[5]Throughout, I use the Anglicized version of this term instead of the more original Greek "hegemon."

Geopolitical Lessons from the Persian Gulf

The Price of Success

President Bush's mobilization of America and the world to intervene in the Persian Gulf—followed by the swift and decisive triumph on the battlefield—*appears* to represent a victory, not just for American forces, but for the president's concept of a "new world order." This concept itself is subject to two divergent interpretations. One is true multilateral collective security, involving a genuine coalition of nations (though, of course, hectored by American diplomacy), to secure order in every region of the world. Those who have always been affectionate toward world government have been celebrating its resurrection in this action. It may seem that the war has put the seal of approval and inevitability on the heretofore inchoate concept of a coalition of nations, exerting common enforcement power, against an obvious aggressor—in short, the classic regime that I call collective security (as a *system* and a structure of the international system, not merely a series of sporadic peacekeeping initiatives, and epitomized by the UN Charter's Chapter VII and Article 43, on the UN Military Committee, which some now would like to revive, requiring dedicated forces).[6] But even if the Persian Gulf coalition cobbled together by the United States represented true collective security, that type of regime at best is unstable and even self-contradictory and thus chimerical. Certainly, it is demonstrated to be transient historically.[7] Moreover, in the present coalition, what we have is a collection of self-seeking governments

---

[6]Note the article by Brian Urquhart, "Learning from the Gulf," *New York Review of Books*, March 7, 1991. Note also Joseph Lepgold and Andrew Bennett, "Putting Teeth into the New World Order," paper delivered at Georgetown University, April 1991.

[7]See Earl C. Ravenal, "An Autopsy of Collective Security," *Political Science Quarterly* 90, no. 4 (Winter 1975–76): 697–714.

arrayed against a small regional power; none of this provides a true test of a collective security system.

Ironically, an exercise like collective security is most likely to collapse in proportion to how necessary it is. Imagine an Iraq that was a true threat to global security—that could bipolarize the regional conflict (by bringing Israel into the war and realigning the belligerents) and ignite a macroregional and even quasi-global conflict (perhaps ushering in a new "age of Crusades"). However contrary to fact that speculation, it proves the essential point about collective security: if it can be accomplished, it is not necessary; if it is necessary, it will fail or disintegrate, probably in the effort itself (as it did in the Korean War, which was the apogee of post–World War II collective security).

The other interpretation—and in my view, the inner meaning and objective intent—of the American move is that this is an aggressive assertion of American unilateralism, appropriate to the status of the "sole remaining superpower." (Of course, if this action expresses a Bush Doctrine, such doctrine remains as yet unarticulated—perhaps a metaphor for the entire Bush administration. The content of such a doctrine would be that the United States, as the survivor of the cold war, can afford to retrench somewhat in its tangible military power and defense budgets, but still needs to keep a good deal of force and still needs, and deserves, to wield decisive world influence.) The latter interpretation harbors an actual disdain for allies and for the processes of international organization but masks that disdain in the rhetoric and institutions of collective security.

Whether the former or the latter interpretation is correct, the gulf campaign will mark the last gasp of either idealistic American support for collective security or the impulse of expansive American unilateralism. Thus, the events since the Iraqi invasion of Kuwait in August 1990 only *seem* to confirm the common wisdom about American national strategy in the post–cold war era: that, with the waning of bipolar competition with the Soviet Union, American strategy should now be directed to active intervention to resolve other-regional conflicts, among virtually any contestants, on terms favorable to American interests; and that those interests themselves are to be defined broadly and generally, even abstractly, as the maintaining of stability and order in any and every region of the world.

In the months following Saddam Hussein's aggression against Kuwait, American intervention dampened the prior congressional and public intent on a federal budget that would involve serious cuts in the defense program, to a level far beneath present forces and spending. Now these dollars must finance the newly manifest American responsibilities in the world, and American forces must be sized and tailored to implement a newly discovered range of global missions.

But that analysis of the international system, and its implications for American foreign and military policy, are overdrawn and misleading. Disturbances—even severe disturbances of a political-military, not merely an economic or cultural, nature—there will be, in most regions, out to the horizon of time. But they will neither threaten the core values of American society nor in any case respond favorably and durably to American military intervention. Far from indicating a mandatory American political-military response, these disturbances are symptomatic of the regionalization of power—the fragmentation of power both among and within the regions of the world—and therefore the potential self-limitation of regional quarrels. And far from compounding "the threat" to the United States, multiple international and intersocietal rivalries, and even death struggles, fracture and waste and deflect otherwise possible aggregations of potent and hostile force.

Under the circumstances, American policy should be to "quarantine" regional violence and compartmentalize regional instability. But this is not to be done by active intervention. Quite the contrary. Compartmentalization can be accomplished, almost by definition, better through nonintervention than through automatic universalization of the quarrel, which has been the instinctive response of the United States in the gulf crisis. Intervention by the United States in other-regional antagonisms and conflicts— whether unilateral or collective—is the only way that such violence could reach America's shores and heartland or impair the core values and true interests of American society.

At most, American policy should be to encourage regional balances of power, whether bipolar or multipolar. And not necessarily neat and precisely calibrated balances; rough and messy ones will do. Yet, in the case of the Persian Gulf and Southwest Asia, incessant and feckless American intervention not only has, in the past, antagonized and neutralized potentially effective power balancers—such as Iran, which is still the obvious hegemone in the area—but also has, in the present instance, largely preempted the power-balancing role that intraregional countries should perform. American intervention encourages regional countries to hang back (though perhaps placating urgent and personal American presidential appeals with small or even token gestures of cooperation) and watch the Americans do the geopolitical work they should be doing for themselves.

What goes for the United States goes also for the other erstwhile superpower. Instead of aspiring to joint intervention along with the United States, in some condominial compact, the Soviet Union should join the United States merely in a bargain not to intervene— a mutual nonintervention pact, if you will, but tacit and fortified only by cumulative example. Mutual nonintervention would remove the suspicion that one or the other was deliberately trying to "make a profit" by intervening in some regional situation, whether by taking sides or just by interposing its arbitration or good offices.

More conflict and less determinacy within other regions of the world would not—contrary to prevalent perceptions—create more danger and less stability in the entire international system or in the immediate precincts of the United States (though that judgment applies less comfortably to the Soviet Union). Rather, the isolation of conflicts within other regions, regardless of how those conflicts were resolved or not resolved, would contribute to a kind of "metastability" of the entire international system—that is, a situation where even extreme political fluidity and violent and abrupt change could occur within regions, and yet the structure of the entire system would not be undermined. The payoff is that nations such as the United States could remain neutral and substantially unaffected by disturbances in other regions.

True, there could be serious indirect effects of such other-regional quarrels, such as short-term and even protracted resource denials and excessive price fluctuations of certain commodities. Those possible effects will have to be envisaged and in some way provided for, but they will not be profitably provided for by preparing for military intervention.

A pertinent example is the fact that American preparations for military intervention in the Persian Gulf, ostensibly to protect the oil flowing to the United States from this region, are "worth" $196 to $266 a barrel—in addition to the price of the oil.[8] Better to allow the market, acting in anticipation and fear of resource denial, to discount all risks and to provide incentives to hedge against such denial, through diversification and substitution and other contingent arrangements.

In the course of a war, its objectives, various and ill-defined as they might already have been, further change—and even become somewhat circular, in that the conduct of the war narrows down to ending it as soon as possible on "favorable" terms. But it is still important to discern what we are, or were, fighting about, in order to figure out what the real comparison of costs and benefits is and whether, in terms of that equation (or "inequality"), there is any net advantage in undertaking this *kind* of operation.

In other words, there must be a "so what" factor, consisting of both a stake and a calculus of the costs and benefits of intervention. Only if we perform such intellectual operations can we draw lessons from an encounter and usefully apply our history to our future. I discern that, in the case of the Persian Gulf—putting aside the not entirely dysfunctional rhetoric and sentiment about world order—the war is for oil or, more generically, "access to resources."

Thus, we have to compose a calculus to determine whether, after the smoke of battle has cleared, it was necessary or advantageous to have prepared for and fought this war—and so, in the future, others that might look somewhat different but will have similar "dimensions." That calculus is not altered by the success of the gulf war. I judge that this war for resources has been unnecessary—or, more precisely, will be seen to have been unnecessary—and, from an overall cost-benefit standpoint, unprofitable, and therefore should be, not the first exemplary instance of its kind, but the last instance of its kind, and that, in the post–cold war period, the United States should not prepare, at great expense, to wage this kind of war.

I make that judgment for three reasons:

---

[8]This is a refined recent estimate. For an elaborate discussion of the costs and benefits of the Persian Gulf intervention, see the quantitative analysis and citation of sources later in this paper.

1. The comparison between the military insurance costs of oil and the differential value of the oil, if undefended, is unfavorable; it costs us more to "protect" the oil than to "lose" it.
2. Any political or geopolitical objects that we gain in that region of the world will be transient, unless we are willing and able, as a society, to stay there "forever," which our society is not structured and disposed to do.
3. There is an alternative, and that is to leave regional situations alone, with the aspiring hegemones and their possibly destructive and immoral conduct—leave them, that is, to regional antagonists and other power-balancing "antibodies." In other words, our intervention in such regional quarrels is unnecessary because such quarrels are self-limiting and will burn themselves out before they spill over dangerously into other regions, particularly our own.

As the real lessons of the gulf seep in, even the successful war will be seen as merely another piece of evidence of the problem of disintegration of power, not a harbinger of the solution. Then, America's choices will be narrowed again and will converge on the acceptance of mutual disengagement. Mutual disengagement (for all its implications of not entirely benign neglect of the world) will become the indicated course of security for both waning superpowers. The events of the gulf are an early warning of a new state of affairs in the world, to which nations, even the erstwhile superpowers, will have to adjust, rather than pursue their illusions of control.

Constructive Generalization

Therefore, we must look beyond this war and derive some guidance for larger U.S. military policy—not just in the Persian Gulf, but toward other regions of the world.

The United States has won the war of its choosing. This is an impressive accomplishment and a compliment to the competence of our military commanders and planners, earlier casually maligned by the press, the public, and assorted politicians and analysts. If you have to have a war, this is the right way to fight it.

But some of the official and popular lessons of the Persian Gulf War—starting the day of the cease-fire—are skewed. The mood of the public and most commentators is that the lopsided American victory over Iraq not only wipes out the disabling lesson of "defeat" in the Vietnam War—the so-called "Vietnam syndrome" that has been the incubus of a generation—but presages worldwide acceptance of American dominance. President Bush has been basking in not just 90 percent domestic popularity, but extravagant judgments by other national leaders about his place in history.

What did this war do? It refuted—and should shut up—the more superficial critics of the past. The "military reformers" are deservedly hurt for impugning American commanders, planners, and operational doctrines (for their supposed preference for "firepower and attrition" over "maneuver"); American weapons (supposedly too complex); and the emphasis on logistics and management (to the supposed neglect of strategy and combat leadership).

But most of the larger conclusions being drawn are the result of misreading the past and, therefore, unreliable as guidance for the future. First, about "reversing" the Vietnam experience: America did not "lose" the Vietnam War in any ordinary sense; it simply fought an elusive and frustrating enemy and tired of the war. In other words, the American political system "decided" to quit. No force—certainly none in the Third World—could "defeat" American arms then, any more than now. Therefore, it did not take the Persian Gulf to disprove and reverse Vietnam; complementarily, the Persian Gulf does not prove the reverse of Vietnam—namely, that the United States can and ought to have license to apply its arms and the threat of its arms to the rest of the world and reestablish its power and determinative influence in other regions of the world.

The real lesson of Vietnam was that, precisely because of the way America fights—with overwhelming forces, state-of-the-art weaponry, and heavy logistics, not so much substituting firepower for maneuver, quality for quantity, or management for tactical brilliance, but trying to "have it *all*"—American wars are inevitably expensive. More than that, preparation for all future wars must be inordinately expensive too, in terms of steady-state "peacetime" costs. The Persian Gulf *reinforces* that lesson.

America will not be defeated on the battlefield. But the price of success is very high and is to be measured in the perpetual cost of creating and maintaining our kind of force structure and panoply of weapons—to support our kind of operational doctrines, to implement military missions that represent a national strategy of global

17

intervention, and in turn, to cement a foreign policy of dominance of various future coalitions to enforce universal collective security. All this cannot be done just by proclamations or even by boycotts and embargoes, unless they are enforced. Even then, the successes will be transient. The victories will come unstuck, and new challenges will arise in the regions of the world: virulent regimes, assaults on friends, manipulations and strangulations of resources. In the longer run, the price of success will be rejected by the American political-economic-social system.

Of these things, too, the Persian Gulf is an example. Perhaps the most ironic point—overlooked in the proverbial "fog of battle"—is that, when the fog has lifted, Persian Gulf oil will still cost the United States $196 to $266 a barrel in military insurance costs alone, not even counting the price of the oil. At the height of the war, the United States had on the battlefield, around the gulf, about 45 percent of its worldwide active force structure:[9] 10⅔ ground division equivalents (9 Army and 1⅔ Marine) out of 21; 18⅓ tactical air wing equivalents (9 Air Force, 6 Navy, and 3⅓ Marine[10]) out of 44; and 6 Navy carrier battle groups out of 14. Although that deployment was more than the forces normally (and now, for FY 1992) attributable to that region's defense, even the latter can be put at 4 ground divisions (3 Army and 1 Marine), 9 tactical air wing equivalents (4 Air Force, 3 Navy, and 2 Marine), and 3 Navy aircraft carrier battle groups. And those forces normally kept for a Persian Gulf contingency cost about $50 billion a year.

This interpretation of the Persian Gulf does not say that the United States—or more properly, its constituent individuals and groups—has no "interests" in other regions of the world; only that some interests cost more to defend than they are worth. This will be as true in the future as it has been in the past. Therefore, success in the gulf does not counsel the assumption of global military obligations. Rather, it indicates an attitude of realistic weighing and objective "indifference" to intervention in all but exceptional cases. It advises our encouragement of regional balances of power by indigenous nations alone, the quarantining of regional quarrels, and an American posture of strategic disengagement.

[9]Units still in the active force structure as of February 1991.

[10]Actually, 1⅔ double-strength wings; Marine air wings, organic to the fighting division, are virtually double-strength in terms of fighter-attack aircraft.

It takes nothing away from the tactical brilliance of the American military victory in the gulf—or for that matter, from the adroitness of America's diplomats in assembling and preserving the coalition of disparate nations in the face of their diverse motives—to say that, actually, on August 2, 1990, President Bush and his advisers "panicked" (at the opportunity no less than at the threat) and pointed the entire country, and a large part of the rest of the world, toward a pretty "big time" war to save the oil resources of the Persian Gulf from the Iraqi dictator. We have to return to an examination of the propriety of that reaction, as a species of the kind of campaigns that America—now fortified by its victory in the Middle East—is preparing to wage, and the general stance that America is encouraged to take toward the world.

Two larger things are likely to happen that might make the initial taste of efficient victory turn to ashes. First, such victories come unstuck in time, in far-off regions (not necessarily along our own borders, of course). The only way to "nail down" a region is almost literally to nail down and sit on the lid of the coffin forever. In general, we must provide the peacetime force structure and budget dollars, on a high, sustained level, for such probable periodic operations. True, there may be some relief through the commandeering of resources and the "bandwagoning" support of regional countries. But eventually, the countervailing factor of local resentment and hatred will make our presence intolerable, for them and for us. Thus, the cost, even of success, is military and economic overextension and eventual political exhaustion.

Second, the incidence of that cost becomes quicker in an era of pervasive public information and public expression. What happened to the United States in Vietnam will also be characteristic of the present U.S. victory and future such victories in other-regional battles. Making the force of our arms stick will exhaust the patience and the limited tolerance for sacrifice of the American people. To say that the United States "lost" the Vietnam War is merely a convenient, but misleading, shorthand. After all, in the narrow military sense, the Viet Cong Tet offensive in 1968 was a victory *for the United States*, as were the Air Force and Navy bombing campaigns over North Vietnam. But sufficient parts of the enemy forces evaded defeat and destruction (perhaps the secret of their survival was that they did not know they had been beaten), and so, the war went on, and eventually the American policy process hived it off. Thus, the important lesson of Vietnam was not dumb bombs (or dumb generals), black pajamas, or an incompetent ally.[11]

Those are the points that have to be made before we construct new defense programs: not just what we want to do in the world, but how amenable the regions of the world will be to American intrusion on cost-advantageous terms, and how amenable the American people will be to a series of expensive and transient victories. The answers, over time, to these larger, more general questions must be negative. And so, to prepare future defense programs on the premise of global intervention, even in some individually feasible and honorable causes, and against some disreputable enemies, is not wise policy.

We must look for large alternative policies, objectives, and strategic principles to guide the sizing and tailoring of America's military forces. That is not what we are seeing in the Bush administration's FY 1992 defense program.

What would such an alternative principle be? It may be that, for a half-century, we need not even have contained the Soviet Union's probes into the Third World. But, leaving aside exercises in revisionism, now, after the disintegration of the Soviet empire, regional imbalances will not reliably redound to the credit of a potentially global adversary; therefore, we should not attempt or prepare to rectify such imbalances with military force. Rather, we should allow—even encourage, in ways that might present themselves to us as simple and neutral—regional balances of power or distractive contests within regions. In other words, our maximum objective in other areas of the world should be to contain disturbances, but not through military intervention.

[11]See Earl C. Ravenal, *Never Again: Learning from America's Foreign Policy Failures* (Philadelphia: Temple University Press, 1978 and 1980).

The Future Shape of the International System

The large parametric condition that is changing is the international system. This is not a complete abstraction, but an analytic expression that describes the entire network of effective interrelationships among the major participants in global politics, mostly in its political-military (not its economic) dimension.

However one classifies international systems (and internal methodological disputes persist within the discipline—or indiscipline— of international relations), one can usefully describe anything from a dichotomy to a dozen types of international system, structurally different in ways that are meaningful and operational.

I differentiate the possible types of international system as (1) unitary "empire"; (2) collective security—not a series of more-or-less effective peacekeeping operations, but a coherent system; (3) bipolar confrontation of alliances; (4) multipolar balance of power; and (5) the limiting case, what I call general unalignment, which happens to be the fragmented array of some dozen or dozen and a half nations that, I believe, now impends.

The world, which already passed from bipolarity to multipolarity some 21 years ago in the early regime of Nixon and Kissinger, is now on the brink of a further transformation—to a state characterized, structurally, by extreme fragmentation of political-military alignment and by the regionalization of power (and the variegation of regional situations within what many have, up to now, in a carelessly undifferentiated way, called the Third World).

The international system is changing in ways that invalidate even the modes of discussing and analyzing situations in the world, particularly military alliances, as well as modifying the situations and institutions themselves. A pertinent example is NATO—over its 42 years not only America's preeminent political-military commitment, but the badge of loyalty and responsibility, and even balance and sanity, within the foreign affairs community. (Those who dissented from the consensus on the essentiality and permanence of NATO came to understand the force of what I call "the sociology of foreign policy.")

As late as January 1989, it was plausible for even such a detached observer as Professor Robert W. Tucker, who had sketched out (though not quite vis-à-vis Europe) the notion of "A New Isolationism,"[12] to opine:

> So long as the structure of the international system retains even approximately its present form, the United States and the Soviet Union are fated to be rivals. Their rivalry may vary considerably. Indeed it already has done so, though the future may find still greater change in the direction of moderation. But so long as structure is not essentially transformed, the rivalry will persist. And so long as it does, there is no reasonable alternative to a Eurocentric policy for the United States. That policy is so apparent a response to interests that it persists despite all the differences and the inequities that have come to mark the alliance. It persists because any of the suggested alternatives—whether they take the form of a Pacific orientation or of a global unilateralism or, more likely, of a hemispheric isolation—would inescapably result in a dispersion of the power that has been the foundation of postwar order. This is why even resolute critics of the Atlantic alliance rarely call for a change in policy that would in fact sacrifice the American interest in Europe. And it is why visions of an alternative to a Eurocentric policy appear either vague or confused when the infrequent attempt is made to translate them into coherent policy.[13]

But it is precisely that essential condition—"so long as the structure of the international system retains even approximately its present form"—that is changing, and was changing in January 1989, under the surface of the situation. (If professors of international relations have any utility, it should be in prying under the surface

---

[12]Robert W. Tucker, *A New Isolationism: Threat or Promise?* (New York: Universe/ Potomac Associates, 1972). See also the review article, Earl C. Ravenal, "This Way Out—A Radical Alternative to Intervention," *Washington Post*, July 16, 1972, Book World section.

[13]Robert W. Tucker, "Reagan's Foreign Policy," *Foreign Affairs* (America and the World 1988/89) 68, no. 1 (1989): 19.

of events and configurations and discerning the potential for, and the imminence of, important structural change.)

If spring is indeed approaching, the ice floe will be breaking up. Where, along what fault lines, will it crack? Into what pieces? The system that appears most probable in the midrange (the next 15 to 30 years) is what I call general unalignment. This system goes beyond the present, controlled multipolar balance of four, five, or six powers. It is characterized by a more extensive fragmentation of power and political-military initiative; by a variety of power configurations in regions of the world, from hegemony to blocked hegemony and a more even balance of nations; and by somewhat wider nuclear proliferation. It is a system that occurs if several important nations pursue minimal involvement, or if power becomes sufficiently diffused to allow autonomous political-military behavior by more than perhaps 8 or 10 states. In short, this will be a world of regional powers.

Several other points about the impending international system should be understood. It will be a state system, recognizably and operationally. Indeed, some of the present tendencies to regional integration, such as Europe 1992, will be frustrated on the political level (but not quite defeated, of course, because such integration delivers efficiencies in various pragmatic arrangements among nations—economic, environmental, informational—and these tendencies will continue as a counterpoint to the reversion to more traditional power relationships). To a certain extent, traditional balance-of-power arrangements will reemerge in the regions, though not in the international system as a whole.

And power—though its functional components might be effective in altered mixture—will still be the crucial determinant of a nation's status and role in its regional configuration and, in some cases, in the global system. Indeed, power will still be composed mostly of political-military factors, though it will not always rest in the same proportion on the purely military factor, as opposed to some economic, social, and even cultural factors. Such "other functional" factors can become more important in defining and supporting power, though they will not replace it.[14]

[14]See the inventory of factors of power, in a section by that subtitle, in Earl C. Raveral, "National Strategy in the Future International Order: Notes toward a Theory of Non-Intervention," *Small Wars and Insurgencies* (forthcoming).

Using indices based on year-2000 population and present gross national product (GNP), military personnel, and military spending, then modified by other, qualitative indices, one can project an international system composed of some 27 important countries in the various regions, playing several kinds of roles.[15]

For the future time frame of 15 to 30 years, hegemonic powers (not in order and not all unopposed, of course) will include the United States, China, Japan, and the USSR; another tier consisting of the rising regional countries, Indonesia, India, Nigeria, Iran, and Brazil; and a list of ponderable though doubtful contenders, Vietnam, Germany, South Africa, and Egypt. Counter-hegemonic powers will be the more obvious ones, Pakistan, France, Israel, and Argentina; and perhaps a few of the less obvious or more doubtful ones, Mexico, Canada, South Korea, Australia, Bangladesh, Britain, Sweden, Saudi Arabia, Syria, and Iraq. This list, though derived from orderly criteria, is more indicative than definitive of the actual individual nations; yet it is definitive of the whole future international system. This system and its actors are described in Table 1.

The Regionalization of Power

Although the regions of the world will become more important, this does not mean—as in the popular conception—an increasing emphasis on the Third World. The term "Third World" will be less useful as a descriptor of anything that is operational and significant to the foreign policy and strategy of the important nations. What will matter is the particular power configurations in the regions and how they come together in the global system. (The regions, moreover, will include non–Third World areas such as North America and Western and Eastern Europe.)

The Third World will not only be a lexicographical misnomer; it will also not be a lake in which the great powers can fish in an undifferentiated way. Would-be extraregional intruders will find various regional situations; in some cases, they will find rising regional hegemones, perhaps not entirely capable of dominating their own regions, but at least capable of preempting their own regions by resisting and rebuffing external intervention.

[15]These summary conclusions are spelled out and supported in Earl C. Ravenal, *Beyond the Balance of Power: The Future International Order* (forthcoming).

Table 1
PROJECTED HEGEMONIC STANCE OF NATIONS

Region	Present or Putative Global Power	Probable Regional Hegemone	Doubtful Regional Hegemone	Regional Competitor or Counter-Hegemone	Doubtful Competitor
North America	United States				Mexico Canada
East Asia	China Japan				South Korea
Southeast Asia		Indonesia	Vietnam		Australia
South and Central Asia		India		Pakistan	Bangladesh
Eastern Europe	USSR				
Western Europe			Germany	France	Britain Sweden
West and Middle Africa		Nigeria			
Southern Africa			South Africa		
Middle East and North Africa		Iran	Egypt	Israel	Saudi Arabia Syria Iraq
South America		Brazil		Argentina	
Total	4	5	4	4	10
Total with hegemonic potential	13				
Total with counter-hegemonic potential				14	

In the future international system of general unalignment, there will not be superpowers, in the same sense and to the same extent as in the present and past. The United States and the Soviet Union themselves will increasingly be confined to their own regions, in political-military terms. That is, they will become regional powers or at most macroregional powers. Predictably, the United States will remain the leading power, but it will not be able to translate that primacy into much usable political-military influence beyond its own region. The Soviet Union (or some Russian federation) will remain the second most powerful nation in the world, though somewhat amputated. But that proposition does not absolve the Soviet Union of future confrontations, because, in its own multiple regions, it will have essential competition—preeminently in Northeast Asia, where a triangular balance will establish itself, without the United States, among Russia, China, and Japan.

One must not be overly impressed by the almost-metaphorical power of loose and even internally antagonistic groupings based mostly on economic convenience, such as the European Community (EC). And one must have severe reservations about the status of Japan—not only its ability to translate its surplus productivity, industrial discipline, technological virtuosity, and accumulated capital into political-military stature and influence, but also its ability to maintain its present momentum in those very economic aspects. A united Germany should be classified, for the future, as a doubtful regional hegemone. It can (and probably will) usefully *support* the Soviet Union, but it cannot subdue it. And Germany's pretensions will again be countered by a vigilant, though not overtly antagonistic, France, which will again move to build its own coalitions in Eastern Europe.

Qualitative Aspects

From a "qualitative" standpoint, what will be the characteristics of the emerging international system, within which, more than upon which, the foreign policy of the important nations will have to operate? We can identify six critical conditions.

The first is the high probability of troubles, such as embargoes, expropriations, coups, revolutions, externally supported subversions, and thrusts by impatient irredentist states.

The second tendency is increasing interdependence, but it has a different implication from the one its proponents would recognize. Interdependence is a set of functional linkages of nations: resources, access routes, economic activities and organizations, populations, and the physical environment. Those areas harbor problems that could be aggravated to the point where they became threats to the security of nations, demanding, but not offering, solutions.

The third element of the future international system is the probable absence of an ultimate adjustment mechanism, in the form of a supranational institution that can authoritatively police the system, dispensing justice and granting relief. Of course, some organized cooperation among states will occur; but the situation described here expresses the structural fact of a lack of hierarchy in the future international system.

A fourth factor is an interim conclusion of the first three: the actions of states to bring about conditions in the external system that enhance their security will take the form of unilateral interventions rather than collaborative world order. (This is not to say that such interventions will be advisable or effective or that the present superpowers have not begun to learn from the frustration or the disproportionate expense of such ventures.)

The fifth future situation—the heart of this analysis—is the diffusion of power beyond some ideal geometry of powerful but "responsible" states. By all measures of power—military (nuclear or conventional, actual or potential), economic (total wealth or commercial weight), or political (the thrust to autonomy and achievement)—there may be a dozen and a half or even more than two dozen salient states, not necessarily equal and not necessarily armed with nuclear weapons, but potent to the point of enjoying the possibility of significant independent action. The diffusion of power has several aspects. One is that limits become evident in political unions, and cracks appear in military alliances. Another aspect of diffusion is the likely impracticality of military power, whether nuclear, conventional, or subconventional—specifically when used to attempt dominance from a distance. (This is not, however, to assert either the absolute or the relative disutility of military force, particularly if one contestant has this force and another does not.)

The sixth condition that will complicate the enforcement (collective or even unilateral) of international order is the incoherence of domestic support, not just in our country but to a certain extent in all. The lack of public support might not prevent interventions, but it might critically inhibit their prosecution. (This, I take it, is the enduring lesson of Vietnam.)[16]

Nowadays, with the disintegration of the communist world, it is frequently suggested that future threats to the security of the United States will come from nonmilitary and even nonpolitical sources and causes. This amounts to a dual assertion: (1) that the nature—the "functionality"—of threats will change and (2) that the new kinds of threats will be peculiarly virulent and dangerous to the United States.

The first claim is true, but not precisely in the sense in which it is put forth. First, granted, instead of the familiar vista of concerted armed attacks by the Soviet Union and its main regional proxies against America's treaty allies or other clients, we will see other-functional threats arising from a matrix of economic causes, environmental factors (such as global warming, air and ocean pollution, ozone depletion, and massive deforestation), population-based problems, and "social" phenomena such as terrorism and narcotics. But the effective form in which such other-functional problems manifest themselves will often be attempts by regional powers to *use* them for *strategic* purposes (a familiar example is deliberate resource denial or embargo), thereby elevating them to the level and import of militarily and politically aggressive designs. In other words, there will be considerable "spillovers" of these other-functional problems into political-military areas. There will also be the usual primary political-military thrusts, such as the attempt to incorporate ethnic minorities in other countries through exercises of force and sheer attempts to alter national boundaries. These will perhaps eventuate in some regional conflicts, even nuclear conflicts.

A second point is that, despite the "salience" of such other-functional issues, the structural and political-military questions of who governs and what is the shape of the international system (who

---

[16]See Earl C. Ravenal, *Never Again: Learning from America's Foreign Policy Failures* (Philadelphia: Temple University Press, 1978 and 1980). Few societies will hold together in foreign exercises that are ill-defined or, contrarily, dedicated expressly to the maintenance of a balance of power. Indeed, the Nixon-Kissinger administration did not cultivate active, fervent public support; acquiescence would have been more appropriate for a subtle, flexible balance of power policy—as long as it was limited to the faint demonstration of force. But if escalation were required to validate an earlier measure that was indecisive, support would be lacking, and the intervention might fail before it had achieved its effect.

has the power, how it is regulated, and what rules of international conduct are built into the foreign policies of the essential nations, the system-consisting and system-maintaining nations) are still decisive for international relations—that is, *definitive* of the system.

The second implication of the currently fashionable claim—that other-functional disturbances are especially threatening—is exaggerated. True, those troubles are vexing and frustrating. But the overall point is that, in terms of the responses to be made, those other-functional threats that are *not* elevated to the strategic level through the deliberate policies of states—that is, those that remain on their own functional level (and this pointedly includes narcotics)—are not prime candidates for the use or preparation of military force. And even those other-functional threats that are elevated to strategic significance (such as politically directed embargoes or terrorism orchestrated for real military effect) are not such that they require the types and magnitudes of military preparation that we have been accustomed to over the past four decades. Perhaps, on a low, constant level, some more vigilant passive defense should be considered, but that is all.

In other words, despite the salience of such other-functional issues, the ubiquitous, multifarious, and apparently ineradicable threats that loom on the horizon will be, on the scale of grand strategy, nuisances, reminders of the increasingly stultified police role of the erstwhile superpowers. This situation may be nasty and brutish, but it will not be short.

Axes of Conflict

A predictive survey of the regions of the world does not disclose an even pattern. There will be hegemones, or would-be hegemones, of a wide variety of capabilities and innate power. And a variety of situations will result. There may be a few situations of uncontested dominance; but more likely, there will be some degree of contest. Regional antibodies either already exist or will arise, still sometimes aided by extraregional countries. The result could range from successfully contested dominance with perpetual pairs or groups of antagonists to anarchic situations without clear determination or pattern. All could erupt sporadically into conflicts of various intensities and natures.

In fact, all the situations involving the most significant emerging Third World regional powers—India, Brazil, Indonesia, Iran, Nigeria—are characterized by some degree of contest and blocked ambitions of hegemony. All of these regional hegemones or would-be hegemones are obstructed by regional competitors or coalitions, or at least by natural geographical limits that define their subsystems of dominance. Brazil is opposed by Argentina and perhaps a wider encircling coalition. India is opposed by a still potent, even resurgent, Pakistan and now has a not-friendly Bangladesh on its eastern flank; it also has China to its north. Other emerging, as well as established, powers are bounded by opposing nations, aided by geography.

An enumeration of potential axes of regional conflict would include India-Pakistan, India-China, Vietnam-Thailand, Vietnam-Indonesia, Indonesia–Malaysia and /or Singapore, Indonesia-Australia, Philippines-Malaysia, North Korea–South Korea, Ethiopia-Somalia, Uganda–Tanzania and/or Kenya, Nigeria-Zaire, South Africa–(more radical) black African coalition, Egypt-Israel, Syria-Israel, Iran-Iraq, Iran-Saudi Arabia, Iraq–various Arab gulf states, Iraq-Syria, Algeria-Morocco, Greece-Turkey, Brazil-Argentina (with others), various pairs of Central American countries, USSR–some Eastern European country, and USSR-China.

Many of these situations would present temptations or compulsions for extraregional powers to intervene. The scale of intervention might start with the limiting case of diplomatic support and proceed through economic assistance, arms deliveries, training and technological infusions, supplementary forces such as air and naval units, and, ultimately, ground forces.

Whether nations consider such interventions to be wise or constructive will depend not entirely, or even primarily, on the circumstances of the individual case and the particular national interest involved—however it might appear on the surface of the matter. This is the practical fallacy of case-by-case analysis. Intervention will depend more critically on the more general norms that nations apply to themselves and on a more general calculus of the productivity of intervention (its preparation, its execution) within the overall framework of the future international system.[17]

[17]And on certain "deep cognitive" dispositions, inherent in the decisionmaking system, regarding the probability, discounting, and relevance of threats. These "strategic cognitions" operate across the board.

Implications for Security

The regionalization of power, the end of the facility of extra-regional intervention, is the impending state of affairs. What are the implications for the security of the great powers, especially the United States? In particular, what are the implications for strategies and defense programs (forces, major weapons systems, operational doctrines, and number of military personnel and cost)?

We cannot just leap from a projection of the world, with its threats and disturbances and axes of conflict, to responses, in terms of anticipated deployments of forces, and therefore defense budgets. There must be some linkage, some objective demonstration of dangers *to us*; then *principles* for strategy; then functions of forces, major missions that forces might have to perform. Only then can we design the forces themselves—and even then, only subject to economic-political-social constraints, resulting in almost inevitable shortfalls.

First, the grander aspects of strategy. We have here not merely a choice among policy alternatives but literally a choice of worlds— alternative states of the international system, held as the largest objects of the foreign policy of the significant powers. But, since international systems are also the environment in which foreign and military policy will have to be made, they also operate as determinants—mostly as a set of constraints—of the foreign policies of nations, especially because they are largely outside the control of the nations themselves.

At the present juncture, for the first time in half a century, both the United States and the Soviet Union have a chance to plan their strategies and military forces, not exclusively and obsessively with reference to the strategies and forces of the other, but with reference to the changing parameters of the entire international system. Thus, it is of cardinal importance for each side to understand where that system is going—not next week, but over the broad span of the next 15 to 30 years—and to view the international system with

31

sufficient perspective, even abstraction, to discern its emerging structural outlines. For, to an extent not readily grasped by those "making" military policy in the United States (and the Soviet Union, too, though its present preoccupation with internal affairs obscures most of the outlines of any foreign policy it may be entertaining), the keys to the future lie in understanding—and accommodating—the evolving shape and characteristics of the international system. This is true even of the erstwhile superpowers, who enjoyed substantial autonomy from the pressures of lesser countries and indulged themselves in the conceit that they were immune from the constraints of the international system in the large—indeed, that their actions, together certainly but even singly, could alter and shape the parameters of that system. (But that, of course, is the definition of a superpower.)

The basic choice that presents itself to the superpowers is between (1) the continuing or renewed attempt at control and (2) a modest adjustment to the workings of the international system. Increasingly, both waning superpowers will have to take the international system as they find it. The shape of the entire system—as well as the conduct of its individual members—is moving beyond the determinative reach of either power (and these two have certainly been the only countries in the past half-century that could plausibly be called superpowers, in the operational sense of powers whose writ runs far beyond their own immediate region—indeed, whose decisions can definitively alter the very shape of the international system).

To validate that assertion, some methodology is required. One must have some systemic perspective—even theory—of what defines and determines an international system and what are the ideal and the actual alternative states of that system. I describe five different types, or states, of the international system. At this juncture of history, I discern that only two of these are available to the two superpowers, as objects of their policy.

History is properly seen as the unfolding, the endless shifting, of the parameters of the international system, which is mostly a political-military universe. It was a shift of the system of parametric conditions that caused the first realization, by both superpowers (mostly unnoticed in the flurry of renewed cold war preparations) in the early 1980s, that competitive intervention in the Third World was not only increasingly inhibited and frustrated, but also unnecessary and unproductive. It was perhaps a dual realization by the new Soviet leader in 1985—that (1) there was no profit in winning the Third World and (2) the United States was not the inevitable enemy or even competitor—that prompted him to explore an accommodation with the United States.

More surprisingly, there was a parallel recognition on the American side in the early Reagan administration—earlier, I would insist, than commonly realized. The brief history—the essential failure— of the Reagan Doctrine played its part in this.[18] The Reagan Doctrine (articulated—or not—in 1985) was part of the entire Reagan administration's attempt to restore American dominance in the world, more or less the way it had existed (in reality or in nostalgia) 25 or 30 years before. But even this cheap and wishful policy of revanchism at the periphery of the communist empire proved to be ephemeral, because it was unmanageable, unprofitable, and consequently politically unsustainable. And this is not to mention the main defense policy, which aggregated weapons, fleshed out force structures, and raised defense budget authority to a peak of $350 billion a year in constant 1991 dollars. But this, too, had already occurred by the midpoint of the Reagan administration, in FY 1985.

The Reagan policies failed largely because they strained the fiscal and "moral" resources of the American people. Thus, the effort at American restoration had peaked, psychologically and morally (as peaks go, without too many people noticing), by the time of the administration's request for the 1983 defense budget; though it did not peak, in constant dollars authorized by Congress, until two years after that. But before its midpoint, the Reagan administration had already begun to explore an accommodative stance toward the Soviet Union.

The efforts of the Reagan administration—now hailed in some circles as the burst of demonstrable strength that brought about the final capitulation of the communist world—turned out to be, in my estimation, another "bend point" in post–World War II American

---

[18]See an account of the Reagan Doctrine in Earl C. Ravenal, "The Reagan Doctrine in Its Strategic and Moral Context," *Small Wars and Insurgencies* 1, no. 1 (April 1990): 22–38.

foreign policy.[19] Ironically, precisely because the Reagan administration tried so ambitiously and still failed, it provided, despite
itself, another piece of evidence that the age of the superpowers—
both superpowers—is passing.

The important point in the somewhat grudging retrenchment
of military effort in the United States, and the more precipitous
retraction of the Soviet Union, is not that they proceed from some
imaginative vision of collaboration in making and keeping peace—
as seemed to be the case at the free-wheeling, almost manic Reykjavik summit of October 1986. Rather, what is important is the
operation of the objective constraints of the international system
and of the domestic political economies of the two contestants.

The workings of these two sets of factors can be seen in three
substantive areas of the policy agenda of the superpowers, in
which, during the 1980s, mutual accommodations had to be made.
The first was, of course, arms control. The second, equally obvious,
was some kind of disengagement from Central Europe—a truce
between the alliances, a settlement of the German question, a putting back together of Europe. Third was a modus vivendi regarding
intervention in the so-called Third World, that playground of the
displaced ambitions of the two cold war contestants; this would
have to apply even to Leninist fraternal internationalist assistance.

The first area, arms control, was, in my view, an easy target for
agreement, since the requisite formulas were straightforward, the
area was subject to the exercise of rationality, and the essential
interest of the two parties was demonstrably common—that is,
the elimination of those combinations of arms that created crisis
instability, which is the only avenue to a possible nuclear war
involving the homelands of the two powers. And so, as it turned
out, arms control was and is achievable (despite the trailing edges
of the Strategic Arms Reduction Talks and the treatment of research
and development of strategic defense).

[19]The earlier important point of deflection of the course of American foreign policy
and national strategy was the Nixon Doctrine (writ large, as the Nixon-Kissinger
move from unsupportable bipolar confrontation to the more subtle and more efficient
multipolar balance of power). See Earl C. Ravenal, *Large-Scale Foreign Policy Change:
The Nixon Doctrine as History and Portent* (Berkeley: University of California, Institute
of International Studies, 1989).

The second area, the adjustment of positions in Central Europe, has been resolved in its essential direction by history and the will of peoples, though practicalities and institutions must still reflect the changes. Although the situation was subject to intelligent initiatives from the Soviet side (Gorbachev's sweeping retrenchment of Soviet power in Central and Eastern Europe), the initiatives were more accommodations of reality—which does not render them any less constructive or imaginative. What is less evident, but also now in train, is that (under the cover of Soviet acquiescence in unified Germany's membership in NATO) the United States, too, is being pried out of its geopolitical position in Europe.

The third area has been more intractable: competition in the Third World. Yet there, too, both parties have been responding to the lessons (though imperfectly learned)[20] of Vietnam and Afghanistan and other situations: the shifting and unsound basis for political allegiance; the transience of any gains, political or military; the exemplary ingratitude of clients; the grossly unfavorable cost-benefit ratio of intervention; the bottomless pit of economic aid; and finally—and most important, because it is a structural factor—the rise of self-sufficient and powerful regional hegemonic powers, suspicious and resentful of extraregional penetration.

In a much-noted observation, a century and a half ago, the political analyst Alexis de Tocqueville foresaw that Russia and America "each seemed marked out by the will of Heaven to sway the destinies of half the globe." De Tocqueville was, of course, clairvoyant: something like this did happen between the 1940s and the 1990s. And so the 20th century can be aptly designated, not precisely the American Century (unless one intends this in some grand cultural sense, including styles of economic behavior), but rather the Age

[20]In the case of the Persian Gulf, both the United States and the Soviet Union are continuing to experiment with various forms of intervention. The Soviet Union, under Mikhail Gorbachev, has been using active diplomacy to gain independence from U.S. direction, preserve the internal authority of its own union government and Gorbachev's presidency, and reinstate its influence in a contiguous and unstable region. Those are objectives that are more tangible and more understandable than those of the United States, which has been using expensive military force to promote global collective security, to extend its reach into an area halfway around the world, and to affect the price of a commodity for which it could more efficiently pay more or substitute.

of the Superpowers. Yet de Tocqueville was not permanently correct, for it is precisely the age of the superpowers that is coming to an end.

Now, the large options afforded to each of the waning superpowers—in terms of alternative international systems taken as objects of their foreign policies—are twofold. The first is to attempt—as did Brezhnev and Nixon in 1972 and 1973, and as Gorbachev has been offering to do with Presidents Reagan and Bush since Reykjavik in 1986—to achieve condominium. This would have to be seen as a collusion to rescue the declining domestic fortunes and international status of both superpowers. It is an intelligent response and a real option; but it is not, I would judge, the main current of history.

The other alternative, mutual disengagement, is more likely, precisely because it is more the product of the objective realities of the unfolding international system. This unfolding change can be identified as the fragmentation and the regionalization of power—to the point where extraregional intervention by the great powers is rendered unproductive on the one hand and unnecessary on the other. In this context of general unalignment, the appropriate foreign policy orientation is strategic disengagement, which I have long advocated as a unilateral, even if unreciprocated, move by the United States, and which now becomes a stance available to both superpowers.[21]

[21]See Earl C. Ravenal, "The Case for Strategic Disengagement," *Foreign Affairs* 51, no. 3 (April 1973): 505–21.

The So-What Factor

It appears, then, that the prevalent threats in the future international system will be peripheral to the United States (that is, other-regional) or not directly strategic (that is, other-functional). What should be the response of the United States?

American foreign policy and military programs, especially over the past half-century of the cold war, seem to have had two programmatic characteristics: (1) they have been fixated on "threats" as, in a superficially logical way, a sort of reason for action; and (2) when committed, they have been—again, quite plausibly—committed to the waging of "successful" operations. Something like that has again happened in the Persian Gulf. Even in a ground encounter, and even with the large forces committed, the United States is fortunate not to be able to do worse than bloody its own hand. And, like a business foray into a given market, well executed against formidable competitors, the American campaign is a success, within its own terms. Yet the success itself may be irrelevant to the larger, appropriate business of the enterprise and, in some later era, may even advisedly be hived off.

The point is that a nation's strategies should emanate from its fundamental situation in the world. Traditionally, the United States has been a neutral and has combined—in only a semblance of inconsistency—self-contained, "continental" geopolitics with the economically and culturally open borders of a great trading nation. This is not the formula of isolationism, in the sense of the hermetically sealed Japan under the Shogunate for three centuries. This extreme version has never been an option for the United States. Rather, in its characteristic periods, the United States has realized the strategic advantages cited by George Washington in his Farewell Address of 1796: America's unique geographical situation and its essential immunity from the noxious ideological quarrels of the older worlds. At most, the United States would be content to benefit from global and other-regional balances of power, as it did in its own nation building in 1776 and 1812, and throughout the 19th century, until the radical consequences of the Spanish-American War of 1898, which marked America's emergence onto the stage of world power.

What this means is that this country (as all significant countries) must evaluate the world's problems in terms of two related questions (the two ends of the telescope): What do the problems mean for our position in the world? And conversely, and perhaps more important, what does our position in the world mean for our evaluation of the problems? It is these so-what questions, rather than the more apparent "what" questions, that should dispose our foreign and military policy.

In other words, before threats can be translated into strategic tasks, we must examine that intermediate term, the so-what factor. Indeed, an account of the so-what factor will constitute part of a theory of intervention—that is, of the propriety of intervening and the propensity to intervene.

There is a tendency, in large-scale projective studies of intervention (which, in their own way, are the president's State of the Union message and the secretary of defense's posture statement), to formulate objectives in somewhat abstract terms (for example, power balances almost for their own sake or moral goals that propagate our values). Sometimes such studies (mostly those on the critical side) formulate principles to regulate intervention (procedural norms pertaining to conditions for collaborative action, sanctions by international organizations, discussions in particular forums).

But more important are (1) the *stake* in regional situations with regard to some real referent, such as the security of the potential intervening country, and (2) the *calculus* by and in terms of which the choice will be made. The stake and the calculus together constitute the so-what factor, the reason for intervening. There must be something in the prospective outcome of a situation (more precisely, the "differential outcome" between the results of intervening or abstaining) that engages the attention and concern of the potential intervenor and "makes sense" in terms that can be measured (at least in principle), in some sort of a calculus, against the costs of intervening. This so-what factor is a bridge between the situation itself and the response of the intervenor. It provides the answer to the operational question: is the case compelling to the point of intervention or counterintervention, or is it on the borderline of indifference, or is it below that borderline, in the area of nonpropensity to intervene?

The stake can be spelled out more concretely in some possible conditions for concern (I do not intend the following ones to be my normative choices, and this is not a comprehensive or definitive list):

- Support of the regional power by the other superpower or another significant power;
- Alignment with the other superpower;
- Threat of economic damage through embargo or simple incompetence (such as mismanaging canals, oil fields, mines);
- Damage to our values (democratic, humanitarian) in some way that seems essential;
- Violation of some procedural rule of conduct that has a "world-order" significance or the creation of a damaging precedent;
- Military threat to an ally or friend or a threat to the integrity of an alliance;
- Direct threat to some strategic object—some choke point, strait, canal, or route of access;
- Threat by a regional hegemone to become a new global competitor or to eliminate or displace a present global competitor;
- Too rapid, or discontinuous, expansion or aggrandizement of a regional power.

Some such factors or aspects must be present in the situation. Otherwise, no connections will be drawn between external events and the action or reaction of a large extraregional power. The situation will be, from the start, a matter of objective indifference or less. And any action taken will be a non sequitur. (The stake and the calculus of costs and benefits provide the "sequitur.")

The behavior of the regional powers (more autonomous, independent, and capable) and the messiness and "softness" of regionally contested situations will themselves be the most important impediments to superpower intervention and, by extension, to the possibility that, if our own self-restraint were not reciprocated, a competitor, such as the Soviet Union, would correspondingly profit from our reluctance to intervene. This, in turn, will be the primary factor that transforms the present system (still a modified balance of power dominated by a few great sources of power with global influence and reach) in 15 to 30 years into a system characterized by a more even distribution of *effective* influence on situations (though not necessarily of raw power in its rudimentary and first-order indices).

The regional powers will accomplish this not by directly challenging the great powers but, quite to the contrary, by transforming their regional situations. This they will do by observing local bounds for their aspirations and limiting the spillover of their quarrels, exercising enough political-military initiative to assert independence from the more distant larger powers and enough power within their regions to preempt large-power intervention. In "systems" language, regional situations will present potential extraregional intervenors with a "tilting" of the cost-benefit equation/inequality. In that kind of projected situation, the larger powers, including the United States, might find it both more costly to intervene and less necessary or advantageous to intervene. They themselves might lapse, residually, into a more regional status and posture.

How much difference might that make? Admittedly, the abstention of a powerful nation, such as the United States, from the defense and enforcement of "justice" or order might seem to produce regions that were either war ridden or dominated by mighty, uninhibited, and immoral states. But a diffuse international system would limit the confident and efficient expansion of a would-be hegemone. It could scarcely hope to dominate more than its immediate region or subregion, and how this would constitute a danger to the essential interests of the United States remains to be proved.

A changing international system transmits itself to, and reflects itself in, the choices of the individual powers, because each nation, in the last analysis, calculates its security, and the elements and requirements of its status and welfare, against the actions contingently necessary to preserve and enhance these values. Nations respond to this calculus, not to some abstract balance of power over and above its tangible, individual security significance; not to some altruistic commitment to *other* nations' structures of costs and benefits (or "schedules of utility"); not to some selfless concern for values in the world outside their own practice and enjoyment of those values; and not to merely economic stakes, as long as these remain "transactional" and do not rise to the strategic level. And in terms of this calculus of strategic interests within the framework of the parametric factors that constrain the pursuit of those interests, even the larger powers are finding that domination or control, or even effective influence, outside their own regions is passing beyond their reach.

This is a truly strategic way of looking at national choices—taking into account international and domestic constraints and costs in determining national responses. It will be an increasingly appropriate way of viewing our choices in a world that will be characterized by tighter and more rigid parameters and will offer a narrower field for the pure initiative of any power. This orientation is suggested by two key questions:

1. Can we live with the existing or probable state of affairs—with what other states are likely to do, without the intrusion of our force or coercive influence?
2. Can we get what we want within acceptable costs and risks?

These questions indicate the lower and upper bounds on our actions. And they will probably cause us, as well as other large powers in the world, to acquiesce in, rather than attempt to dominate or control, other-regional situations (and even countenance a few breaches in our own regional sphere).

The Example of the Persian Gulf

Real Defense, Real Costs

I have said that there has to be a *criterion* for intervention, not merely some disturbance or potential "threat" in the world. In other words, there must be, not merely a "what" proposition—a factual description of some trouble somewhere, however vivid and even unnerving—but also a so-what factor, including a stake and a calculus of the costs and the differential benefits of intervening or abstaining (somewhat modified by certain cognitive orientations). The latter two elements constitute, roughly, a nation's propensity to intervene.

In this regard, high on the list of objects of American foreign policy that are often declared essential—and thus, if threatened, occasions for military intervention—is the Persian Gulf. This region stands as a surrogate for the whole question of our assured access to resources—in this case, oil—that are held to be virtually irreplaceable on acceptable terms and are subject to interdictions by powers and factions inimical to the United States and its interests.

It is in this broad sense that we take the Persian Gulf as an example—not necessarily as the problem looked before America's recent intervention, and certainly not mandatorily as it may look afterward, but as it should look *generically* as a category of possible future U.S. intervention.

No doubt the oil of the Persian Gulf is a serious matter. But expressions of the importance of an interest do not entail our extending military protection of it. This is not to deny the interest. Neither the interests nor the threats are fictitious. But they are not absolute or infinite, either. Interests must be weighed; responses must be compared. Proposed actions must be arrayed against each other and against inaction.

Whatever the propriety of defending the Persian Gulf (and this question is far from being decided or adjudicated, in particular or in general, by the fait accompli of our military intervention,

Operation Desert Storm), undertaking the defense of such a "new" area—as the United States did in January 1980 in the Carter Doctrine, which specified and militarized a commitment that, insofar as it had existed before, was only implied and mostly political—is not cost-free.

So the cost of a doctrine that commits the United States to defend a new region is inevitably incremental. Commitments may be articulated in fine phrases, but they must be implemented by forces. In the case of the gulf, for the end of FY 1992, the U.S. baseline, or peacetime, forces primarily attributable to the category that encompasses the Central Command (CENTCOM) (which pivots on the Persian Gulf), "Other Regions and Strategic Reserve," account for 6⅔ land divisions (5 Army and 1⅔ Marine) out of 17 land divisions (14 Army and 3 Marine) in our force structure, 14⅓ tactical air wing equivalents (7 Air Force, 4 Navy, and 3⅓ Marine) out of 39 tactical air wing equivalents (21 Air Force, 12 Navy, and 6 Marine) in our force structure, and 4 Navy aircraft carrier battle groups out of 12 in our force structure. Thus, that category, Other Regions and Strategic Reserve, takes 39 percent of the cost of our general purpose (other than strategic nuclear) forces, which cost $215 billion—or $84 billion. The portion attributable to the Persian Gulf is roughly 60 percent of that category, or 4 land divisions (3 Army and 1 Marine), 9 tactical air wing equivalents (4 Air Force, 3 Navy, and 2 Marine), and 3 Navy aircraft carrier battle groups—coming to $50 billion.[22]

So the issue of costs cannot be escaped. The question, then, is not whether it would be nice to have continued access to Persian Gulf oil on tolerable terms. Rather, the question is whether it is feasible to fight for that oil if access to it for ourselves (or conceivably for our Western European and Japanese allies) is threatened by some local, regional, or extraregional aggressor, and therefore, derivatively, whether it makes sense to prepare, perpetually and at great expense, to do this.

---

[22]This baseline, peacetime, force structure for the Persian Gulf is to be distinguished from the actual emergency or wartime deployments at any given time. For instance, as of mid-February 1991, 10⅔ division equivalents (9 Army and 1⅔ Marine), 18⅓ tactical air wing equivalents (9 Air Force, 6 Navy, and 3⅓ Marine), and 6 Navy carrier battle groups were in the Persian Gulf area. Those actual wartime deployments represented a larger fraction of our worldwide active force structure.

A Conceptualization of the Problem

How do we decide the question of the propriety of defending the Persian Gulf?[23] The feasibility of this proposition can be assessed only by presenting a calculus, in terms of "expected losses," of the contrasting courses of action or inaction: to protect access to oil by American armed intervention or to "let" the region and the control of its resources slip into the hands of an aggressive regional power or (more pertinent in an earlier time) the Soviets or their proxies.

There seemed to be, on the eve of the forcible American intervention in and over Iraq, some doubt among Americans about the stake—what the United States was about to fight for in the Persian Gulf.[24] Yet, upon cool analysis, it seems that the current (as well as some previous) American intervention in the gulf represents the critical instance of using or threatening force to defend our "access" to an important resource (implicitly on "reasonable" or "tolerable" terms). Put another way, the oil rationale (both price and absolute access) may easily furnish a necessary condition for American military intervention and may constitute in itself a sufficient condition,[25]

---

[23]The defense costs of oil depend on what factors one includes, as well as how one estimates the costs of those factors. The costs here are newly calculated. Earlier estimates were made in Earl C. Ravenal, "The Strategic Cost of Oil," testimony before the Subcommittee on the Panama Canal and the Outer Continental Shelf, Committee on Merchant Marine and Fisheries, U.S. House of Representatives, June 27, 1984; "Defending Persian Gulf Oil," *Intervention* (Winter 1985); "Doing Nothing," *Foreign Policy* (Summer 1980); "Persian Gulf Oil," syndicated radio broadcast of October 20, 1987, in Cato Institute, *The Best of Byline 1987* (Washington, 1988); and "The Case for Adjustment," *Foreign Policy* (Winter 1990–91). For a different calculation, see Alan Tonelson and Andrew K. Hurst, "The Real Cost of Mideast Oil," *New York Times*, September 4, 1990, Op-Ed section.

[24]See "Vox Populi: Winds of War," *Washington Post*, December 23, 1990, Outlook section, in which "only" 31 percent said that "to lower oil prices" was a good enough reason to make war with Iraq. That is a somewhat different proposition, of course, from a straight empirical judgment of what the administration was actually fighting for—and, admittedly, part of a multivariate equation, including such other independent variables as "to prevent Iraq from ultimately attacking Israel," "restoring the former Kuwaiti government," "preventing Iraq from controlling a larger share of Mideast oil and threatening the U.S. economy" (actually a reinforcement of or addition to the "to lower oil prices" rationale), and "preventing Saddam Hussein from threatening the area with chemical and biological weapons."

[25]This is not to say, however, that the administration got the calculus correct—or perhaps it would not have intervened or prepared to intervene, at least in the way it did.

45

whether or not other factors are present. Thus, the current interventionary crisis in the gulf is paradigmatic of one large category of American interventions, mostly in the Third World, that is likely to outlast the end of the cold war.

More concretely, in the case of the Persian Gulf, I assert that on the one side—the "left-hand side"—are the military costs to the United States of warding off (by deterring or defending against) threats to our access to some or all of the Persian Gulf oil. On the other side—the "right-hand side"—is the differential impact on us of our doing something or doing nothing—that is, the effect on us of a presumably successful maintenance of the normal oil flow, less the effect on us of losing whatever actual quantity of oil or whatever price advantage in oil we consider to be at risk.

That is the basic relevant calculation, to be done in *aggregate* terms. As a kind of alternative expression, or excursion, it is also interesting to calculate the left-hand side of the equation—that is, the military costs to the United States of warding off threats to our access to some or all of the Persian Gulf oil—in terms of the military costs *per barrel* of oil that we consider to be at risk.

At first glance, one might want to take just the bare present yearly cost of defending this area, in peacetime, with no calculus to reflect possible wars. But that cost would be too low because it leaves out two important surrounding conditions.

First, we must not just take the current cost of generating forces for this region, but reach into the intermediate-term future—say, 10 years out—and account, in some way, for the rising costs of those forces. We must compound for probable cost escalation. Defense costs generally leveled off during the mid to late 1980s, after their relentless rise over the decade from the end of the Vietnam War in 1975. Thus, it would be conservative to take no real cost increases and only 4 percent per year for inflation. The full annual cost of our forces for the defense of the Middle East and Southwest Asia—so-called CENTCOM—is $50 billion. Compounding at 4 percent for 10 years, then averaging over that period, we arrive at an annual cost, to generate and maintain forces for that area, of $60 billion.

Second, we must account in some way for the admittedly amorphous costs of possible wars of various types. We are interested in representing the "steady state" of meeting the contingency in question, which we may be trying to deter or, if it happens, counter. One way to trap such costs is to consider the possible cost of the kinds of wars that could be incurred by our assuming the defense of this area—in the case of the gulf, a conventional and a nuclear war—and assigning an additional probability that each might happen within, say, a 10-year period.

Thus, the more precisely refined statement for calculating the left-hand side is (1) peacetime military preparations, taken as the present portion of the defense budget attributable to defending this region for, say, 10 years, compounded each year by a percentage comprising the projected real increases in defense spending (if any) and the expected rate of inflation; plus (2) the expected loss in a regional conventional war; plus (3) the expected loss in a nuclear war.

To arrive at the expected loss for each kind of war for the 10-year period, we will multiply the contingent cost or damage of each kind of war by the probability (expressed as a decimal fraction of incremental probability) that such a war would eventuate from America's commitment; then, we will divide by 10 to arrive at an annual expected loss for each.

The conventional war is not such a distant and improbable event, after all. But instead of figuring the incremental costs of the actual war in the gulf—and even these are difficult to conceptualize, let alone quantify—we are interested in a more generalizable kind of number. Therefore, we take as the wartime costs only the incremental defense-budgetary costs, because destruction to the American homeland would be virtually nil. The speculative figure that I have chosen is a "half-Vietnam-size" (not necessarily Vietnam-length) war—less extensive in time but correspondingly more intensive in violence and destructive commitment of force per area of conflict. The Vietnam War cost, over its many years, about $350 billion, all costs included, but would now be perhaps three times as much, or about $1,050 billion.[26] Half a Vietnam-size war, then, would cost $525 billion. The incidence of such a war during the decade under consideration might be 10 percent more probable because of our

---

[26]The ratio of defense budgets: 1992, $278 billion, over 1975, $93 billion.

commitment to defend. This will yield $5.3 billion a year expected loss.[27]

For a nuclear war, we take (for obvious reasons) not merely the cost of American military assets, but an estimate of the damage of such a war to American society. A plausible expression might be the loss of GNP over the extended period of time that such loss would affect the American economy. Here we will find, of course, that the absolute damage that such a war would cause is enormous; yet the additional adduced probability of generating a nuclear war against some adversary, as a consequence of our taking on the defense of the Persian Gulf, is minuscule. That added probability might be taken as ¼ of 1 percent. In considering the devastation to the United States as a consequence of being hit by a nuclear strike— averaging out the types and weights of nuclear attack—one might consider that the United States would lose an average of ¼ of its GNP per year, over the 10 years. (This is not even to quantify the human costs of such an occurrence.) Taking the FY 1992 U.S. GNP as $6 trillion[28] and compounding at 6 percent a year for inflation and growth would amount to $79 trillion for the decade. That means the United States would lose $20 trillion of value over 10 years, or $2 trillion a year. Multiplied by the subjective probability factor of ¼ of 1 percent, that would create $5 billion a year of expected loss for the factor of a possible nuclear war.[29]

"Where the Money Is"

To assess the steady-state costs of peacetime military preparation for the defense of the Persian Gulf region, one must begin by determining "where the money is" in the defense budget—that is, what strategic tasks, missions, and functions are responsible for

[27]Over the decade, this would come to $53 billion—not so far off the "actual" cost of the U.S. Persian Gulf deployment and war, Desert Shield and Desert Storm.

[28]The Fiscal Year 1992 *Budget of the United States Government* (Washington: U.S. Government Printing Office, 1991) assumes $6.095 trillion.

[29]Is this a "pseudocalculation," as some have called, say, the quantitative work of Carl Sagan and Richard P. Turco in calculating the "lost productivity of people killed by nuclear winter"? In a sense it might be. But some quantity must be included in the equation to represent this possible cost. And the resultant annual value here is minimal compared with the existent, ongoing peacetime costs of providing the force structure for a Persian Gulf contingency.

48

the major categories and amounts of defense spending.[30] Consequently, I offer an anatomy and a methodology that serve to relate the exactions and expenditures of resources to national strategies and ultimately foreign policies.[31] Such a methodology enables a fairly confident and revealing attribution of defense expenditures to the major components of the military services and, more important—and of relevance here—to the regions we are committed to defend.

A Note on Methodology

In order to identify those forces attributable to the defense of the Persian Gulf, we must analyze and allocate the entire defense budget, by types of forces and by geographical region. It may be useful here to give a more detailed account of the methodology by which I arrive at these numbers. There are two sets of calculations.

In one calculation, the rough number of basic combat units (divisions, wing equivalents, important ships) in each of the four military services (Army, Navy, Air Force, and Marine Corps, splitting off the Marine Corps from the Navy in a manner that captures the Navy overhead devoted to supporting the Marines) is divided into the entire manpower of that service and the entire budget of that service (the latter having been adjusted to absorb its share of defense agencies and defense-wide activities). This first calculation tells us the full annual cost of procuring and keeping each basic combat unit. It is also useful for construing the manpower and budget implications of alternative force structures.

In this calculation we count only *combat* forces as defense outputs. Everything else in the defense budget (first, noncombat units and, second, non-military-service costs such as defense agencies and defense-wide activities) is, thus, considered a support cost or overhead. This ensures that we are calculating "full slices," including all support and overhead, as the real cost of those combat forces.

[30]The notorious Willie Sutton, asked why he robbed banks, replied, "Because that's where the money is." Of course, that might explain why he robbed *banks*, but it doesn't explain why he *robbed* banks. Similarly, one can identify what accounts for the major defense expenditures, though it does not necessarily argue for cutting them. Nevertheless, it might help to have a correct, rather than a fanciful, idea of where the money is in the defense program.

[31]A more comprehensive version of this methodology appears in Earl C. Ravenal, *Defining Defense: The 1985 Military Budget* (Washington: Cato Institute, 1984).

49

In our calculation, we attribute all combat forces either to the "strategic" or to the "general purpose"[32] side of the ledger and then distribute all noncombat costs (that is, all the defense programs that represent support or overhead) either to the strategic forces or to the general purpose forces.

Only two of the program categories, strategic (nuclear) forces and general purpose (conventional and tactical nuclear) forces, are true combat functions or true output categories; thus, we must distribute the other categories over those two, in appropriate measure. When we do this for FY 1992, we find that strategic nuclear forces take $63 billion, or 23 percent, and general purpose forces take $215 billion, or 77 percent.

Now we are able to cost out the general purpose forces attributable to some region of the world. To get the costs of defending each region of the world, we multiply the total cost of general purpose forces by a fraction representing the active land divisions (both Army and Marine) attributable to that region—not just the divisions actually deployed there, but those procured and maintained primarily for contingencies in this region—over the entire number of active land divisions. (Land divisions are the practical and the most accessible measure, and they represent well enough the allocation also of tactical air wings, whether Air Force, Navy, or Marine, and also, roughly, of surface naval forces.)

As late as FY 1991, the Pentagon traditionally apportioned its defensive effort first according to strategic nuclear forces or general purpose forces, and second according to three broad geographical "areas": Europe (which has consisted of NATO and its northern and southern flanks); Asia, that is, East Asia and the Western Pacific; and "Other Regions and Strategic Reserve" (the latter being not reserve units but active units kept in the continental United States for service mostly in those Other Regions; this third general purpose category has included the Persian Gulf/Southwest Asia).

---

[32]We have to determine what part of the force structure is attributable to the defense of the Persian Gulf. It will be a fraction of our general purpose forces (not our strategic nuclear forces): our land divisions, Army and Marine; our tactical air wings (the fighter-bombers of the Air Force, Navy, and Marine Corps [double-strength wings]); and our surface naval forces (and attack submarines), expressed in terms of Navy aircraft carrier battle groups. All of those forces are taken on a "full slice" basis, that is, including their appropriate share of the cost of all support forces and overheads.

That is the breakdown that I will use in this analysis, explicitly splitting out a cost factor from the Other Regions and Strategic Reserve category for the Persian Gulf/Southwest Asia, which is in question in the present analysis.[33]

I judge that, for FY 1992, the Bush administration intends the following regional attribution of a total of 17 ground divisions: Europe—after the significant disintegration of the Soviet threat to the area—7⅓ divisions; East Asia, 3 divisions; Other Regions and Strategic Reserve (including the Persian Gulf), 6⅔ divisions (of which 4 are for CENTCOM).[34]

We can now apply those fractions to the general purpose portion of the Bush administration's original defense budget authorization request for 1992 of $278 billion, of which $215 billion is for general purpose forces. Europe will account for $92 billion. Asia will absorb $39 billion. And Other Regions and Strategic Reserve will take $84 billion, of which about 60 percent, or $50 billion, can plausibly be considered to be for the Persian Gulf (in addition to any supplemental expression of crisis/war cost).[35]

The Right-Hand Side of the Equation

The right-hand side of the large cost-benefit equation (or, more typically, inequality) consists, roughly, of the stakes of the potential conflict or intervention (the stakes, of course, from the standpoint

[33]Recently, Gen. Colin L. Powell, chairman of the Joint Chiefs of Staff, proposed what appears to be a different way of conceptualizing the U.S. force structure in terms of four "forces": a strategic nuclear force; an Atlantic force, including Europe and the Persian Gulf; a Pacific force; and a contingency force (characterized as a force for quick reaction to abrupt crises). A moment's inspection will indicate easy and comprehensible translation of General Powell's four forces into the traditional (a) bipartite division between strategic nuclear and general purpose forces and then (b) tripartite regional allocation plus Persian Gulf breakout, by (1) accepting Powell's strategic nuclear force as he states it and (2) splitting the Persian Gulf out of his "Atlantic force" and stating it rather as an identifiable adjunct to his "contingency force." That procedure is the one I will follow in my analysis. For a report of General Powell's scheme, see "Bush Plan to Cut Forces Scrutinized Amid Crisis," *Washington Post*, December 23, 1990, p. A18. The secretary of defense begins to follow this quadripartite division in his *Annual Report to the President and the Congress* for FY 1992 (p. 4).

[34]Or, on the "new" basis: Atlantic 11⅓ (Europe, 7⅓; CENTCOM, 4); Pacific, 3; and contingency, 2⅔.

[35]Or, on the "new" basis: Atlantic, $142 billion (Europe, $92 billion; CENTCOM, $50 billion); Pacific, $39 billion; and contingency, $34 billion.

of the potential intervenor, not from the standpoint of the situation itself or of the entire world or of some groups of other countries). Most important, what is at stake must be represented, not as a potential favorable outcome that might be achieved by our intervention or a potential unfavorable outcome that might be avoided by our intervention, but as a *differential* between the projected outcome of the situation in question with our intervention (that is, through our doing the act under consideration) and the projected outcome of the situation without our intervention (that is, as the result of our doing nothing). In other words, everything we might expend and risk on the left-hand, or cost, side of the equation is for the sake of improving on the consequences of doing nothing.

In the case of the Persian Gulf, to represent what we would differentially lose by failing to insure what we get from this region, we will take some expression of the costs to American society over the period that such costs would occur—limited here for practical reasons (and without too much consequent violence to the analysis) to 10 years. We will consider the costs to American society as those "caused" by the "loss" of the Persian Gulf oil or, more to the point here, the loss of the certain fraction of gulf oil at risk. In other words, what would be lost if we failed to defend the region and, because of that lapse, something adverse were to happen, such as (1) the political-military takeover or control by some regional hegemonic or quasi-hegemonic state; (2) the effective quasi-monopolistic economic suasion by some regional power seeking to maximize its revenues, demonstrate a point, or inflict punishment; or even (3) that most feared event, until just a few years ago—the domination of the region by some extraregional hostile power, notably the Soviet Union.

David R. Henderson calculates the cost to the American economy and society resulting from the price increase of oil imposed by a monopolist of a significant part of the oil of the Persian Gulf region.[36] Henderson takes this to be a discretionary cutback by a rational and actually otherwise disinterested monopolist, not a total deprivation of the entire oil supply under his coercive control, which would be a much larger amount. Such a revenue-maximizing

[36]"Sorry Saddam, Oil Embargoes Don't Hurt the U.S.," *Wall Street Journal*, August 29, 1990; and "Do We Need to Go to War for Oil?" Cato Institute Foreign Policy Briefing no. 4, October 24, 1990.

production restriction, reducing the pre–August 2, 1990, output of 12.3 million barrels per day (mmbd) to 8.3 mmbd—a cut of 4 mmbd—would support a rise in the worldwide price of oil from the pre-crisis $20 per barrel to $30 per barrel. That $10 increase, multiplied by *total U.S. imports* of oil before the invasion of 8 mmbd (Henderson calls this an ample, conservative figure), or about 2.88 billion barrels per year, comes to about $29.2 billion a year, or about ½ of 1 percent of the current U.S. GNP, which Henderson takes as $5.4 trillion a year. And this impact would get smaller over time, as substitutes emerged.

Of course, Henderson's calculus represents perhaps the most benign calculus of the consequences of failing to defend the gulf. It is the calculation of those who figure that oil in world markets is fungible and even a monopolist of the Persian Gulf oil resources— presumably having exerted this control at some sacrifice and risk in order to realize some tangible benefit to his country—must sell the revenue-maximizing quantity of oil or perhaps somewhat less, but not zero. Therefore, they figure that the United States would lose only the price difference occasioned in all oil in world markets, times its usage of all imported oil. This is a sensible approach, and it certainly yields a minimal dislocation as a result of the United States' doing nothing. But perhaps it misses something; or putting it more forensically, perhaps it does not give enough to the war-hawks to anticipate and partially preempt some of their rebuttal.

Henderson appears to realize that the overall costs to American society resulting from such a monopolistic price increase might well transcend the aggregate price increase itself. But he does not develop that more comprehensive conception of loss in quantitative terms. The effect of Henderson's confining his notion of the impact of restrictive monopoly of Persian Gulf oil to its aggregate price effect on the U.S. GNP might be sensibly close to the mark, but it does tend to slight the more serious case made by the hawks (to the effect that oil deprivation would more severely damage the U.S. economy). It may be that we should give the benefit of some doubt to the hawks and use some surrogate larger figure to represent the cost of the economic disruption and the need to adjust. This would be the cost of a depression, stated in terms of lost GNP for a number of years.

The Aggregate Calculus

Now we are in a position to complete the algorithm that represents the military costs and differential benefits of undertaking to defend the Persian Gulf (or, in other words, of insuring access to our supply of Persian Gulf oil).

The left-hand side is the sum of three kinds of defensive costs:

$60.3 billion a year for generating defensive forces in peacetime
  5.3 billion a year for the expected losses of a conventional war
  <u>5.0</u> billion a year for the expected losses of a nuclear war
$70.6 billion a year total

Now for the right-hand side. Allowing, for the sake of argument, the "hawkish" case that the deprivation of Persian Gulf oil might (in addition to the attendant gross mismanagement of the economy) cause the United States a deep and protracted depression, one could express this as the loss of a part of the value of the GNP—say, 10 percent—over a decade. Taking GNP as $6 trillion a year, and compounding it by 6 percent a year for inflation and growth, we get $7.9 trillion lost over a decade, or $790 billion lost in an average year. If it were put as even 5 to 10 percent more likely—say, an average subjective probability of 7.5 percent—that such would be the consequence of the abdication or default of the United States from defending this region, then one could express the cost of this defensive default as $593 billion of expected losses over the decade, or $59 billion a year.

Of course, the wide swings and the subjectivity of such probability estimates, along with the wide ranges assigned to high-value potential consequences, render this calculus conjectural, almost arbitrary. Yet it has its instructive import: with America's predictable (and some imputed) annual cost of $71 billion to insure this region, set against an ample estimate of expected losses from doing nothing, around $59 billion a year, the grand equation comes out about a wash. Put differently, the net economic value of access to Persian Gulf oil, when all costs are included on both sides of the ledger, is about zero.

The Insurance Cost per Barrel of Oil

America's military costs for insuring its access to Persian Gulf oil can be expressed in an alternative way—in terms of the per barrel cost of defending the oil at risk in the region. That is the principal forgotten cost component of oil. If we have to protect our access to resources with our military means, these preparations—mainly the provision of forces—and, beyond that, a possible war must be included in the cost of the resources. That is the common sense of the business and personal world; we all know that insurance is part of the cost of operating an automobile. But somehow, when it comes to insuring our nation's access to economic assets in the world, our government and most of the public act as if that access were free.

We have already determined the numerator of the fraction in question—that is, the present and contingent military costs involved in protecting the Persian Gulf: $71 billion a year. We now have to conceptualize and quantify the denominator of this fraction: some range that represents the number of barrels of oil at risk for the United States in that region.

The latter is not quite as simple as it might seem at first glance. The figure is not, on reflection, the barrels of oil that originate in the Persian Gulf region and arrive at the United States (exported in tankers through the Strait of Hormuz and through pipelines), now or on the eve of Saddam Hussein's invasion of Kuwait. It is, rather, some expression of what is at risk—in a sense, America's dependence on Persian Gulf oil. One can arrive at such an expression but only with caution and within a very wide range. It can be conceptualized in two ways:

1. Take all of America's oil imports from the entire Persian Gulf region—not the constricted amount resulting from our self-imposed embargo, even if offset by the increased production by Saudi Arabia and the emirates, but our imports from, say, several years ago—as reflecting a "core" dependence on doing our energy business in a certain way. That figure is lower than the actual gross usage of Persian Gulf oil that we had fallen into, through convenience and "normal" commercial cost inducements, by the eve of Saddam Hussein's invasion of Kuwait.

2. Take some fraction—a large fraction, of course—of the immediately pre-invasion consumption of Persian Gulf oil as representing the portion of oil at risk, at any single time, through

55

some adverse action or event in that region. In other words, the entire region would hardly be interdicted in the event of the most likely—in fact, the actual—scenario, a regional quarrel in which one regional power made a bid for hegemony and oil monopoly, or quasi-monopoly, while other regional powers not only opposed such a bid but continued to be (perhaps all the more willingly) suppliers of oil. This rough calculus would apply whether the would-be hegemone and monopolist were Iraq, opposed by Saudi Arabia, the emirates, and to some extent Iran; or Iran, opposed by Iraq, Saudi Arabia, and the emirates.

Either of the above "net" numbers of barrels per year would be less, obviously, than the simple gross amount from this region at its highest recent point. To illustrate the point, let us take for the numerator the aggregate military cost for preparation and for contingent wars as the annual average for the next 10 years: $71 billion. Then, let us provide a basis for the denominator by taking a succession of alternative oil import figures (Table 2).

Thus, one could say of military insurance costs for Persian Gulf oil that a "wide" range, over the 1986 to first-half-1990 period, would be $98 to $338 a barrel. But, using an averaged figure for 1986 and the modified criterion of dependency mentioned above, rather than raw total regional imports, we get a narrower range of

Table 2
U.S. OIL IMPORTS FROM THE PERSIAN GULF

	Actually Imported (Full Dependency)[a]	"At Risk" (Half Dependency)[a]	Military Costs ($/bl)	
			Full	Half
1986 (CIA/*AFJI*)	0.210 ⎫		338	
	⎬ avg. 0.267	wtd. avg.	266	
1986 (EIA)	0.324 ⎭		219	
1990 (EIA) based on 1st 5 mos.	0.723	0.362	98	196

Sources: The more recent oil import statistics are provided by Terry Sabonis-Chaffee of the Rocky Mountain Institute, Snowmass, Colorado. They are based, in turn, on information from the Energy Information Administration, U.S. Department of Energy. The earlier data are based also on information from the Energy Information Administration and from *Armed Forces Journal International* (April 1987), p. 50, which is based on CIA, *International Energy Review* (unclassified).
[a]Billion barrels per year.

$196 to $266 a barrel. This is still a wide range, and the underlying numbers are subject to a good deal of judgmental interpretation. But these figures will demonstrate the magnitude of what we are paying to insure our access to this region's oil. And they are in addition to the cost of the oil itself.

Conclusion

What we can conclude from the foregoing calculus of the value of Persian Gulf oil—if we include everything that ought to be included—is twofold. First, the total insurance cost of a barrel of Persian Gulf oil, added to the bare import cost, dwarfs the apparent current price. Second, in terms of aggregate costs, the total costs of defense and expected losses of war are greater than the total consequences of disengagement from the region. Defending the gulf, with a possible war, costs more than doing nothing and possibly suffering the deprivation of oil. A more intriguing way of putting it is this: if we must ward off aggression, the *net* value of this region to us is zero. In theory, then, defending the Persian Gulf, that obsession of contemporary strategists, ought to be close to our indifference point.

Faced with the large ongoing and contingent costs of defending or occupying the oil fields, we should, as an alternative, allow the market to adopt hedges, such as exploration, more intensive recovery, and research into substitute materials and processes. The costs of these moves should be borne by private organizations and passed along to consumers in the form of prices that recover and reflect the true long-term costs of providing the commodities and services. Without going into the detail of identifying comparative availabilities and meticulous costing alternatives, it should be intuitively obvious that even expensive hedging moves are cheaper than the costs of military defense to maintain access to these strategic commodities.

True, oil is an "interest" and has to be measured and put on one side of the balance. But some national interests cost more to defend than they are worth.

Principles for National Strategy

The payoff of the foregoing analysis should be a set of principles to guide American foreign and military policy. Such new principles are much needed. The cold war, of course, has been declared, at the highest official level of both contestants, the United States and the Soviet Union, to be over. Yet the present moment must still be described as "transitional." Operationally, the cold war will not be over until both sides stop targeting each other virtually exclusively and founding many strategic preparations on the eventuality of coming to the aid of allies against the forces of the other bloc. The missions of the U.S. forces have been somewhat diversified, but basically the same cold war force structure is being used residually for lesser regional interventions.

The Condominium Temptation

The specific U.S.-Soviet relationship is likely to take the shape of either of two now-contending forms of international order: The first is condominium, which is a limiting case of the system of collective security but with an overtone of spheres of influence.[37] This tendency has been described by the Chinese as bilateral "hegemonism" ("contending and colluding," as they put it), and they discerned it as a characteristic of the behavior of the two global giants in the 1960s and 1970s. Condominium carries resonances of the cardinal arrangements of the close of World War II: Yalta, which suggested (in its inner meaning) recognition of each of the two superpowers' geographical spheres; and the United Nations, which rested explicitly on President Franklin D. Roosevelt's concept of the "four [soon to become five] policemen," but practically on the collusion of the United States and the Soviet Union. (When the

---

[37]See the descriptions of the international system of collective security and its variant, condominium, in Earl C. Ravenal, *Beyond the Balance of Power* (forthcoming).

latter prospect soon vanished, collective security was virtually still-born, though many of its particular institutions persisted.) Condo-minium also is epitomized by the bilateral negotiation of a regime of arms control that would be discriminatory toward other powers in the world—whether this regime involves strategic offensive weapons or, more intriguingly, strategic defense.

Understandably, the middle powers of the world, the lesser nuclear powers (in Europe, particularly France; in Asia, particularly China), have been disturbed by these tendencies. The last com-pleted round of arms reductions by the United States and the Soviet Union, the Intermediate Nuclear Forces (INF) agreement, rekindled fears that were reminiscent of the recriminations of French foreign minister Michel Jobert, in 1973, about the Nixon-Kissinger impulse toward détente with the Soviet Union. A prospective U.S.-Soviet agreement on strategic defense—say, on research and testing within structured limits—in conjunction with bilateral arms control agreements that contemplate serious reductions also in the nuclear forces of lesser powers—would have the same worrisome effects.

The Disengagement Alternative

The second, countervailing tendency, toward disengagement and the appropriate international system of general unalignment, is, in my view, the dominant tendency. (Indeed, disengagement represented the net significance of President Reagan's stubborn attachment to the ideal of societal strategic defense, particularly at the Reykjavik summit, though his grasp of the logic of his own position was more instinctive, even subconscious, than deliberate and articulate.) After all, the United States, throughout its history, has tended to a sort of isolationist stance, which could be considered the ultimate form of "damage limitation." The highly intervention-ist orientation of the past half-century, including the enterprise of containment of the Soviet Union, should be seen as a large aberra-tion from this primal stance.

In a prescriptive mode, I would say that the United States and the Soviet Union should avoid the attraction of stemming their putative decline, or even disintegration, and of consolidating their respective power through a last bid for condominium. Such an arrangement would require each of the waning superpowers to police its "own" sphere, and even this task might be overdemand-ing and unproductive, especially since it would bring each into collision with the emerging regional powers in its sphere. Better to accommodate the tendency of the international system to general unalignment and the regionalization of power. This accommodation would suggest, rather than mutual collusion in intervention, mutual disengagement and the shrinkage of both erstwhile superpowers themselves to the role of regional—or, at most, macroregional—powers.

Thus, both powers, the United States and the Soviet Union, should be seeking more fundamental principles of national security, for an era in which the array of threats has become diffuse to the point of being conjectural.[38]

With the waning of the familiar direct threat from the Soviet Union, American strategists and commentators are groping for a new focus for our military forces and defense program. Former hawks seek new missions for largely the same forces (in contrast to the doves, who have usually wanted the same objectives but with lower forces). Examples abound. Former Army chief of staff Edward C. Meyer warns: "If you believe the Soviet [sic] has decreased in its international threat, then the two biggest threats are reunification of Germany, and what that really might mean, and what happens in Japan if they get involved in weapons production and other things like this over time. . . . Japan becoming overly involved in projection throughout Asia in any way, shape or form would have a tremendously destabilizing impact."[39] *Fortune* magazine opines that there will be "four missions worth fighting for: Protect the homeland. . . . Keep the goods moving. . . . Prevent power vacuums.

---

[38]I do not consider *internal* security. I assume that, for the foreseeable future, there are no internal threats to the United States; for the Soviet Union, it is not entirely clear what "internal" will mean. The need to provide extensively for internal security is a marked difference in the requirement of the Soviet Union for military forces. There are two aspects of this. First, the Soviet Union must keep much more of its force structure and military potential within its borders, to deal with internal turmoil. That is clearly something that the United States, with a more legitimate government, does not face. Internal strife could include inter-republic warfare, inter-region civil violence, or the suppression of overt secession. (This is not to say that such applications of force would be well advised or successful.) Second, Soviet forces are already becoming more "territorialized," as the republics assert more control over forces raised in, and installations located in, their own territory. So far, this has applied mostly to ground forces; but it could, some day, encompass air forces and even, imaginably, nuclear forces.

[39]*Washington Post*, November 22, 1989, p. A12.

. . . Promote democracy and punish punks."[40] And the key example is an article by Paul Nitze, in which he espouses not merely the now-obligatory objective of "provid[ing] stability" and "support [ing] . . . order," but an additional, rather bizarre, objective of "protect[ing] [not just tolerating] . . . *diversity*."[41]

A proper approach is to look for principles—general yet practical—that can guide the national strategy of the United States in a world of multiple but diffused disturbances, a world in which there is no direct and collected threat to America's vital interests. This requires, first, specifying the objects of defense and, second, identifying the large-scale functional purposes, or categorical missions, for our military forces. Yet, since the traditional defense-planning algorithms are virtually irrelevant, the criteria of defensive objects and military missions are not so much "necessity" or strict derivation from the cited threats, but rather "appropriateness" to the international system and the situation and status of the nation.

And the values that the American defense program is designed to protect would be the core values of society—the lives and domestic property of citizens, the integrity of national territory, and the autonomy of political processes. They would not include "milieu goals" (that is, states of affairs in the international system or particular regions that are desired for the sake of those states of affairs). The values to be protected also would not include secondary strategic objects or ideological tenets, such as human rights or political and economic principles to be propagated beyond our own borders.

The Role of Military Forces

The functions of our military forces would be threefold. First, they would perform the real mission (though it happens to be the least likely one) of defending the approaches to U.S. territory by land, sea, air, and space. This criterion is not to be translated rigidly into some geographical security frontier—say, down the middle of the Pacific or the Atlantic or somewhere in Central America. Rather, the extent to which we would reach beyond our political boundaries

---

[40]Lee Smith, "What We Really Need for Defense," *Fortune*, June 4, 1990.

[41]Paul H. Nitze, "A U.S. Mission for the '90s," *Washington Post*, May 21, 1990, Op-Ed section (italics added). See also the more expansive version, "America: An Honest Broker," *Foreign Affairs* 69, no. 4 (Fall 1990): 1–14.

and engage a threatening military move would depend on judgments that the threat was (1) directed against us, (2) massive, (3) cumulative, and (4) irreversible (but for our timely intervention). Those constitute more a set of "functional" criteria.

Second, our forces would be designed as "second chance" forces. This criterion has somewhat different meanings in the strategic nuclear force and the general purpose force dimensions. As for strategic nuclear forces, regardless of the attenuation of international threats, we must always keep forces capable of deterring direct nuclear attacks on our homeland or nuclear pressures directed by organized political entities in the world (this criterion extends to regional powers that might pose direct threats of mass destruction through nuclear—or chemical and biological—weapons). Of course, that requisite is far less demanding than the multifarious capabilities required by extended deterrence, the attempt to spread our nuclear mantle over other nations and less-than-vital interests. Yet, since the effect of deterrence consists of the product of the amount of retaliatory force times the credibility of using it (which is roughly equivalent to the propensity to wage war), then, since my concept entails less propensity, I would keep somewhat more strategic nuclear force than we strictly need or intend to use, so that we would deter better and thus have to exercise our force less or less probably. I would not overwork this proposition, but in sizing our strategic nuclear forces, I would, working from the low base of mere "finite essential deterrence," err on the conservative side. This requires retaining strategic deterrence in the form of offensive nuclear forces, though not necessarily the traditional ones; these weapons would be reserved for a second strike at military targets. It might also require maintaining a strong research program in strategic defense, though not building or deploying systems prematurely, from a technological or diplomatic standpoint. (The discussion of an appropriate nuclear strategy is deferred to a following section.)

As for general purpose, or, roughly speaking, conventional, forces, it is important, especially when prescribing a severely low force structure in the first place, not to go below the level or type of forces upon which we would need to rebuild if our benign threat assumptions went wrong, in some massive and potentially irreversible way, and the international system became directly and tangibly menacing. We would want to have maintained a diverse cadre of defensive units and a core of diverse defensive activities to hold vital positions and form the basis on which to rebuild with sufficient speed. This argues against tailoring too specifically for (illusorily) precise missions.

In a radically smaller defense program, research and development should rise as a proportion of the whole. This is part of a second-chance approach. Readiness categories (operations and maintenance) can slip a bit (readiness for what?). But the qualitative technological edge must be maintained because of its longer lead-time. Better to keep burnished the potential to fight effectively on the battlefields of the future, even if present invitations to war are declined.

An Appropriate Nuclear Strategy

The third function of our military forces would be deterrence—but only of attacks or pressures against our own territory, society, political processes, property, and military forces. That mission can be labeled "finite essential deterrence."

An appropriate nuclear strategy for the United States—for both nuclear contestants, the United States and the Soviet Union, for that matter—will not be arrived at by comparing numbers and types on each side, though of course quantities and concrete characteristics are important. Rather, the strategy will be determined by considering the problem of supreme security in an age of extreme fragmentation of political-military authority and initiative. The problem challenges both great powers as they turn away from their exhaustive planning to confront each other uniquely and toward the more generic problem of common nuclear security.

Nuclear armaments are not things in themselves, but they constitute one element ("posture," which goes along with the two "doctrinal" elements of targeting and precedence of use) of nuclear strategy. Within nuclear strategy, the doctrine of targeting (typically, counterforce, countervalue, or intermediate variants) dictates both the doctrine of precedence of use (typically, first or second strike, responding to certain types of attack or prior military situations) and the tangible posture (made up of the numbers of weapons; their kinds and characteristics of range, accuracy, and destructiveness; and their basing and "platforms," with various degrees of survivability). In turn, nuclear strategy itself expresses a larger idea of national strategy and, beyond that, even a "philosophy" of the existent, emergent, or ideal shape of the strategic universe and a sense of a nation's situation in that universe.

I have said that the two waning superpowers and erstwhile antagonists should eschew the apparent attractions of a condominial deal. Such a deal might preserve their roles as nuclear guarantors and dispose either or both to interventions—joint or again competitive, in each other's areas, in no-man's-lands, or each in its own conceded sphere—that could perpetuate the threat of escalation to nuclear warfare. Rather, both still-great powers should attempt to build an overall regime that would obviate exposure to damage. That would counsel policies of mutual disengagement.

Finite Deterrence and Extended Deterrence

The nations would still rely principally on deterrence, implemented by offensive nuclear weapons. But this would be finite essential deterrence designed to discourage another nuclear power's attack on the core values of one's own society: people and domestic property, national territory (and, for this purpose, military forces), the structure of society, and the integrity of the political system. The large nuclear powers should avoid extending their deterrence to cover others than themselves and less than (what the French strategists call) "supremely vital interests."

In turn, those strictures give shape to more specific and concrete advice. Abjuring extended deterrence will obviate counterforce targeting (the use of some fraction of the strategic nuclear force to attack a portion of the enemy's target system consisting of military installations, logistical complexes, command bunkers, and—to put the most important matter last—missiles in their silos), which can be demonstrated logically to proceed from the requisites of alliance commitment and guarantee.[42] Indeed, for the United States, the gravitation to counterforce has been virtually dictated by its adherence to NATO, which has always depended on the U.S. threat of

[42]This important proposition, which is not superficially obvious, is argued in Earl C. Ravenal, "Counterforce and Alliance: The Ultimate Connection," *International Security* 6, no. 4 (Spring 1982): 26–43; and *The Logic and Geopolitics of Nuclear Strategy* (forthcoming).

65

first use of nuclear weapons and the promise of continuous escalation from battlefield nuclear weapons to more potent theater types to final use of its intercontinental strategic force. America's extended deterrence has required the "practical" invulnerability of American society itself to Soviet attack, so that an American president could persuade others that he would risk an attack on the U.S. homeland, or that he could face down a threat to attack the homeland, in the act of spreading America's protective mantle over Western Europe. To limit damage to society, the United States must attempt to acquire both a strategic defensive capability and an offensive counterforce capability, in order to degrade as much as possible of an enemy attack on American cities, either ultimately or in the first instance. Counterforce, requiring hard-target kill capability and a redundance of coverage, is the most demanding of the nuclear missions. It is responsible for the major part of the approximately 7,800 warheads now deployed on American ballistic missiles. And, because of the logic and dynamics of incentives, counterforce derogates from crisis stability.

Refusing to threaten nuclear attack for the sake of third parties will contribute to the quarantining of regional conflicts. Abandoning counterforce targeting will remove the incentive to strike first and further contribute to crisis stability—which itself will become more prevalent as the larger nuclear powers, the present alliance guarantors, reserve their weapons for their own essential deterrence and thus truncate the escalation of regional conflicts. In this way, the abandonment of counterforce targeting (which is logically inseparable from the precedence doctrine of preemptive strike) is reinforced by the avoidance of contextual involvement (which could provide the occasion and the impetus for the vertical magnification and horizontal spread of conflict). Both attitudes would lead to a nuclear regime that does not tip over into war and to an international system in which regional conflicts can burn themselves out.

Promoting Crisis Stability

In a nuclear age, crisis stability (the absence of incentive, at any point in a developing confrontation or conflict, for any party to escalate to the first use of nuclear weapons) is the most that can be achieved and the least that can be settled for—but is all that is needed, since, to have a nuclear war, someone must start it. Either one of a pair of nuclear contestants can strengthen crisis stability by designing the elements of its nuclear strategy—its posture and its doctrines of targeting and precedence of use—to discourage the other's first use of nuclear weapons. The United States can change its posture to eliminate its fixed land-based systems as they become even theoretically vulnerable to a preemptive strike (and not replace them with mobile or multiply based missiles, which only displace or postpone the incidence of vulnerability). This would move the United States from the present triad of nuclear forces to a diad consisting of nuclear submarines and stand-off bombers armed with medium-range air-launched cruise missiles.

From the standpoint of doctrine, to discourage an enemy first strike, the United States should not aim at the enemy's missiles in their silos and thereby provoke him, in a crisis, to launch preemptively. Rather, the United States should adopt countermilitary targeting, developing a list of some 3,000 targets[43] such as naval and air bases, concentrations of conventional forces, military-logistical complexes, and (to the extent possible) arms industries that are relatively far from large civilian populations. (The United States should also not deliberately target cities. This stricture derives from moral reasons but also, up to a point, strategic reasons: if the United States avoids the enemy's cities, it gives him no incentive to strike U.S. cities. Even in retaliation, striking "enemy" populations would make no more strategic sense than it ever has and no moral sense at all.)

As a second point of doctrine, the United States should seal off the temptation to be the side that starts a nuclear war, by imposing upon itself a stringent doctrine of no first use of nuclear weapons. The international legal mechanics of no first use are less important than embodying the intention and expectation of no first use in the tangible weapons systems and actual doctrines of nations. It is also less important to achieve reciprocity in a pledge of no first use, or formal acceptance of the principle in a binding treaty, than it is to expand, even through independent moves, the adoption by individual nations of the stance of no first use.

[43]Or perhaps lower—say, 2,000 or even 1,500—in order to avoid atmospheric effects ("nuclear winter") that could become self-destructive.

In sum, with regard to strategic offense, I am arguing for a *triply* restrained doctrine. The United States (or any other nuclear power) would not use nuclear weapons except (1) in response to a nuclear attack (2) on its own homeland, and its riposte would be (3) confined to military objectives that are not nuclear missile launchers. This nuclear doctrine should be combined with a rigorously interpreted national strategy of disengagement and nonintervention, which would reduce the contextual circumstances in which a nation would ever have to use its nuclear weapons.

Strategic Defense

What about strategic defense? It is axiomatic that sovereign nations have a right to defend their territory and, depending on the nature of the attack, the approaches to their territory by land, sea, air, and—what is at issue here—space. And certainly, in moral theory, we would all be better off if we could dispense with what has been called (though pejoratively and misleadingly) "mutual assured destruction" (MAD) and if, instead, the United States could achieve mutual defense with the Soviet Union, as President Reagan overreachingly hoped in 1983. But the technical conditions for an effective deployment of strategic defense—particularly the crucial item of boost-phase interception—are not likely to be achieved for several decades. Even then, one cannot harbor high confidence in developing and deploying a sufficient weapon (whether kinetic, laser, or particle beam) and in turn overpowering Soviet counter-measures, in particular; installing such a system in space orbit; providing the lift (shuttle or rocket) to emplace a sufficient number of objects (whether weapons themselves or platforms or mirrors); insuring the invulnerability of those space systems against attack and other critical degradation; and devising a reliable battle management system, including the computer programs, in advance of the battle, without having the benefit of comprehensive, realistic testing.[44]

The question of confidence affects the larger question: could we count on strategic defense to the extent of dismantling offensive

[44]The secretary of defense more optimistically projects that a downsized version of global strategic defense, Global Protection Against Limited Strikes (GPALS), could be deployed "beginning in the late 1990s." *Annual Report to the President and the Congress*, January 1991, pp. 59–60.

68

nuclear retaliatory systems? In short, would we bet the country on the Strategic Defense Initiative (SDI)? The answer is clearly no. And in that case, the "synergy" of some strategic defense and a residual strategic offense would render the strategic balance precarious, by creating the presumption of a now-unanswerable American first strike and forcing an adversary to consider, and offset in various ways, such a preemptive disarming strike.

There is also the question of cost. Even the lowest estimates now are close to $100 billion over a decade. High estimates run to $1 trillion or $1.5 trillion over two decades or so. Indeed, without even approaching the deployment of any kind of space-based system, the United States has already, between 1984 and 1991, spent $23 billion for SDI, on research and development alone.[45]

These roughly balanced considerations suggest an off-handed treatment of strategic defense. Technologically, strategic defense may work best if it is kept in a state of perpetual, though fairly vigorous, research; we should ensure that our nation is not "out-flanked" by a potential important adversary on this front. And diplomatically, a U.S.-Soviet strategic arms agreement can accommodate research outside the laboratory, even the testing of key components in space, since negative technical assessments are now so impressive that they have already depreciated the risk of deploying an effective system.

Yet despite its disabilities, the tendency to acquire strategic defense will persist—ironically, for two contradictory reasons. First, as long as the United States provides extended deterrence for allies and other strategic objects in the world, it will require societal invulnerability. But second, at the same time, a strategic defensive shelter—an "astrodome"—might allow the United States to revert to a disengaged stance, with no need or inclination to defend allies or to defend forward.

Some now say that, with the evanescence of the cold war, the need for strategic defense is actually accentuated.[46] That is, with no

---

[45]Charles E. Bennett, "SDI Is No Patriot," *Washington Post*, February 5, 1991, Op-Ed section.

[46]That is the view of the secretary of defense: "Within the decade the continental United States could be in the range of the ballistic missiles of several Third World nations in a world dominated by multipolar geopolitical considerations, rather than the East-West strategic paradigms of the past 40 years." *Annual Report to the President and the Congress*, January 1991, p. 59.

major strategic antagonist to contend with, we now have to deal mostly with "crazy states" (though some more calculating than crazy), such as Libya, Iran, Iraq, and imaginable others. In such circumstances, strategic defense is not only more necessary but also more feasible, since off-the-shelf technology might successfully create the requisite "light" shield. But the residual large nuclear powers can get over (figuratively) our defensive barrier and through our defensive shield. And the new small nuclear powers can get under (literally) by infiltration.

Arms Control

What, then, of arms control? The approach presented here is relatively independent of—or at most parallel to—formal arms control. The precise nature of arms control agreements does not matter as much as the United States' attaining strategic stability vis-à-vis potential nuclear antagonists, through prudent and well-constructed moves within its own competence. Such moves could be informal and unilateral. They would have to make strategic sense in themselves, not just as bargaining chips, and they should not depend on the condition of reciprocity, though that would be helpful. A unilateral program could accomplish several of the specific purposes of formal arms control—particularly crisis stability—and some of the general objectives of having nuclear forces in the first place.

In an independent American strategy of disengagement and conflict avoidance, arms control does have an ancillary role. Not all aspects of arms control are designed to enhance stability; some serve the additional purposes of reducing the cost burden of preparing for war and reducing the contingent destruction of war. These other virtuous purposes should not be excessively traded off against stability. Arms control agreements may be sought across a wide range of situations and functions: significant reductions in the levels of strategic arms; an explicit and mutual pledge of no first use of nuclear weapons; a moratorium on the introduction of destabilizing new weapons systems; a ban on the testing of nuclear warheads in any environment and the testing of new delivery vehicles; treaties to regulate the development of strategic defense technologies and anti-satellite weapons; the establishment of nuclear-free geographical zones; efforts to control the proliferation of nuclear arms, materials, and weapons technologies; the outlawing of chemical and biological weapons; limitations on conventional forces; restrictions on arms transfers; curtailment of foreign military bases and deployments; cuts in overall military budgets; mechanisms for peacekeeping and mediation; confidence-building measures; and legal codes that discourage war initiation and war crimes.

Damage Limitation and Its Implications

Nuclear strategy, as a component of a country's larger national strategy, must aim at damage limitation, in the comprehensive sense of minimizing "expected damage" (which can be defined as the product of the harm that would be suffered and the probability of suffering the harm). In all aspects of nuclear strategy (offense, defense, and arms control), in the pursuit of damage limitation two proximate goals must be sought, and then, as it turns out, a third goal.

The first is damage limitation in the strict sense—the reduction of the damage that could be sustained by the fabric of society, and its end values, mostly through an enemy's attack on one's own homeland. This represents the weight of destruction.

The second objective is crisis stability: the absence of effective incentive, at any point in a confrontation or conflict at a lower level of violence, for any party to escalate to a higher plane of destruction. This represents the probability of destruction.

But the entire logic of strategic arms points up an abiding problem of national strategy, which can be posed in a generic way: Whenever, and to the extent that, a nation such as the United States undertakes to provide extended deterrence—that is, to throw its protective mantle over allies and other clients in a way that evokes arsenals with extraordinary destructive power and that causes the defensive commitment to spill over purely local and conventional barriers, and to do this against adversaries who on their own or through their guarantors can respond destructively against one's own homeland—then that nation, in its strategy at the highest level of potential violence, will be driven to seek damage limitation in the strict sense. It will seek to blunt a potential enemy strike against its value targets (or, in the first instance, against its missiles themselves), and that damage limitation will typically consist of preemptive offense as well as strategic defense. That proposition applies to any enemy (any other nuclear-armed or nuclear-protected state) and to any ally (any alliance commitment in a nuclear context).

Thus, whenever a nation such as the United States extends its deterrence, the two cardinal objectives of strict damage limitation and crisis stability will tend to contradict each other and press toward opposite strategies and force postures. In the experience of the United States, the move to a counterforce nuclear targeting doctrine has been an attempt to realize damage limitation, but that has come at the sacrifice of some measure of crisis stability. The sponsorship of strategic defense has been an attempt to limit potential damage to American society directly, avoiding the question of crisis stability; but it is technically premature, and it invites some practical contradictions of its own.

Therefore, a third objective becomes a requisite of national strategy in an era that is both a nuclear age and an age of anarchy. That objective is the avoidance of contextual links, or what I have called "strategic disengagement." This represents the removal of American military commitment to other regions of the world, a passive attempt to quarantine regional violence, and an attitude of accommodation and neutrality—even to the point of objective indifference to the outcomes of political-military contests in other parts of the world. Such an orientation to the world is the only way to shrink the incidence of the dilemma posed by the first two antithetical objectives, damage limitation and crisis stability. It is the only way to dissolve, though not resolve, the antithesis of the two aspects of damage to American society: the destruction of war and the probability of war.

The Defense Debate

It remains to translate the principles of foreign policy and national strategy into a defense program. The derivation of a defense program proceeds through strategy, military missions, forces and weapons and doctrines, and defense dollars and military personnel.

Proposals for defense cuts have hardly been scarce these past seasons. Even the secretary of defense, the chairman of the Joint Chiefs of Staff, and the individual military services have offered impressive reductions. Roughly since December 1988, when Gorbachev announced extensive unilateral cuts in Soviet forces at the United Nations, and then the following year, when the Soviets' external empire in Eastern Europe broke apart, there has been an outpouring of prescriptions for reducing America's defense budget. These have continued, in the wake of the Persian Gulf War. The flood tide includes former meticulous supporters of extensive military strength, such as once-secretary of defense Robert McNamara, and even former staunch advocates of steep force expansion and weapons acquisition, such as John Lehman, secretary of the Navy under President Reagan. The critical movement also includes former cautious advocates of modest trimming, such as William Kaufmann, as well as, of course, those who have long prescribed larger cuts in force structures and defense budgets. By now, it is not hard to find critics who would cut defense budgets from $300 billion a year to roughly half that figure.

As one who has been advocating $153 billion defense budgets (in 1992 dollars) since 1970, I can regard with some detachment the conversion of many analysts to advocacy of sharply lower levels of forces and spending. But now the critics have a rather dull role. First of all, just about everyone in this game now knows how to count forces and defense dollars—something that, two decades ago, only half a dozen people in the defense community knew how to do.

73

Second, the critics are not driving the process of reductions.[47] In any case, the defense program responds to an objective set of determinants. The program is, as it were, ground between the upper and nether millstones of, respectively, the downward pressure of budgetary stringency and resource constraints and the upward pressure of defensive "requirements" derived from threats to American interests. Normally (or abnormally, if you want to look at the matter that way), the defense budget is squeezed or crushed, in the sense that we cannot afford all that we "need." Thus, there is (in the terms of the Joint Chiefs of Staff) a cumulative "shortfall" in our provision for the tangible defense of American interests in the world.

But now, after the cold war, threats to American interests have become shrunken and diffuse. Indeed, some would say that, in this kind of world, the interests themselves are elusive. But internal fiscal pressures, which are as much a part of national strategy as the calculus of defensive requirements, remain real and serious: federal budget deficits will be running over $200 billion a year for some years to come. So the upper millstone of fiscal constraint is still pressing down while the nether millstone of external strategic requirements is falling away. Thus, defense budgets and military forces will go down, despite the residual skeptics and bureaucratic stonewallers in the administration (and some in Congress who would like to preserve parochial pieces of the defense program, such as local bases and industry, many of whom take the gulf war as a pretext for postponing the inevitable cuts in defense spending).

[47]Among other things, the defense critics have concentrated mostly on the wrong targets. The Defense Department habitually complains about "micromanagement," referring to the detailed ministrations of Congress. There is also such a thing as "microcriticism." I use this term to refer to the "military reformers" of yesteryear, and to those avengers of "waste" in procurement whose attention has been attracted to such singular items of hardware as monkeywrenches, stepladders, claw hammers, and toilet seats. Of course, it would have taken a pile of toilet seats to add up to $300 billion defense budgets. The rest of the money must have gone *for something.* Attributing high costs to waste, and performance problems to some demonstrably wanton instances of overdesign, never accounted for more than a tiny fraction of what was wrong with the American defense program: why it cost so much in peacetime, why it sometimes appeared to fail so prominently in wartime. The remedies derived from such critiques were correspondingly unreliable. And perhaps worst of all, the predictions of performance in battle were as wide of the mark as Saddam's SCUDs.

74

Third, it is fair to observe that most critics' arguments for cutting defense spending are entirely circumstantial; that is, they depend on the decline of the threat, or sometimes, as the case is made in more technical terms, the lengthening of warning. The emphasis is now on strategic or even political warnings, which by their nature are much longer than the previous mere tactical warning—a common example being the former putative capability of Soviet forces in Germany to wage a large war from a standing start.

Thus, there is little that is fundamental in most current cases for lower defense preparation.[48] In other words, in both the critics' cuts and the administration's reductions, there is not much policy. Foreign policy has to do with the orientation of a nation toward the international system—both a nation's objective situation in the world and what that nation wants to make of its situation. Thus, of course, policy should be responsive to the situational realities. But there should also be some theme in a country's orientation to the world, not just a series of shallow existential responses, whether on the upside or on the downside.

Even before the cold war was "over"—indeed, *instead* of the cold war—this country might have had a noninterventionist foreign policy, an alternative to containment. Now that we are moving to a less capable military force, we could convert that circumstance into a more permanent stance—a real policy or national strategy— that is noninterventionist. Such a noninterventionist policy and strategy would be a large-scale and long-term response to parametric shifts in the international system.

Yet, to be fair, in the Bush administration's conservative approach to the defense program, there is something at stake on the level of policy—though perhaps only implicitly. A reasonably large military structure *is* (contingently) necessary for the United States to continue to wield global influence, even in a postcontainment phase. The administration represents, fairly though crudely, an enduring majority of Americans who would like this country to play several

---

[48]A rare exception—a defense policy analysis that is based on, and calls for, real changes in national strategy—is Ted Galen Carpenter and Rosemary Fiscarelli, "Defending America in the 1990s: A Budget for Strategic Independence," *America's Peace Dividend: Income Tax Reductions from the New Strategic Realities*, Cato Institute white paper, August 7, 1990.

sorts of global roles, perhaps as the "sole superpower." Critics (such as myself) who opt for a drastically reduced force structure are also opting, wittingly or not, for a much-reduced American role in a much less controllable world.

Force and Budgetary Planning

We are concerned with what would have been spent on defense, what will be spent, and, alternatively, what should be spent. A reasonable swath of time for making those comparisons, and a period for which we can develop relevant figures, is the seven fiscal years 1990 through 1996.

As our point of departure, we have the projected defense budget authorizations of the incoming Bush administration in its requested program for FY 1990 through 1994 (allowing a further consistent projection through 1996).[49] That will give us a baseline for calculating both the subsequent reductions by the Bush administration and concurrent congressional action, and my own recommendations for even further cuts to accord with a noninterventionist foreign policy and a strategy of disengagement.

The "original" Bush defense program would have required, for FY 1990, $296 billion in budgetary authority; 2,121,000 military personnel; a general purpose force structure that included 21 land divisions (18 Army and 3 Marine), 25 Air Force tactical air wing equivalents, and 14 aircraft carrier battle groups with 13 Navy tactical air wings; and the standard triad of strategic nuclear forces. The military personnel and the force structure would have remained constant through FY 1996, and the 1996 defense budget, in current (then-year) dollars, would have amounted to $381 billion. Over the

[49]Secretary of Defense Richard B. Cheney, Statement Before the House Armed Services Committee, in Connection with the FY 1990/FY 1991 Amended Budget for the Department of Defense, April 25, 1989, along with the news release "Amended FY 1990/FY 1991 Department of Defense Budget," April 25, 1989. Those two documents are to be read in conjunction with the outgoing Reagan administration's FY 1990 defense budget: Secretary of Defense Frank C. Carlucci, *Annual Report to the Congress, Fiscal Year 1990* (Washington: U.S. Government Printing Office, January 17, 1989).

seven years from 1990 to 1996, this program would have produced cumulative defense costs of $2.361 trillion.[50]

Now, a plausible projection of the defense program by FY 1996, based on the administration's own anticipated budget requests and on the assumption that, from now on, Congress will tend to accept the now more moderate requests of the administration, is $283 billion (in current dollars); 1.7 million military personnel; and a force structure of 15 land divisions (12 Army and 3 Marine), 15 Air Force tactical air wings, and 12 aircraft carriers with 12 Navy air wings, in addition to a nuclear triad reduced by a strategic arms reduction treaty. Taking the actual performance of the Bush administration, which reduced its initial anticipated requests and further acquiesced in congressional reductions in FY 1990 and FY 1991, and reflecting its present and now-estimated requests through FY 1996, I calculate that those seven years of defense programs will have totaled $1.964 trillion. Thus, the present course of decisions will have delivered, over seven years, savings of $397 billion, compared with the projections of the incoming Bush administration in 1989.

Yet the present Bush defense program provides a global interventionary force structure and harbors a still-expensive commitment to something called NATO. In contrast, a noninterventionist defense program, by FY 1996 (taking the actual expenditures for FY 1990 and 1991 and starting further cuts only in FY 1992), would cost $187 billion (in 1996 dollars, allowing 4 percent annual inflation,

[50]All defense budget figures used in this study are for budget authority (not outlays) for the subcategory 051 Department of Defense (not the entire category 050 National Defense, which also includes 053 Atomic Energy Defense Activities [mostly production of nuclear warheads in the Department of Energy] at $11.8 billion for 1992 and 054 Defense-related Activities [mostly civil defense and the standby maritime fleet] at $.8 billion for 1992). The figure also excludes the added deployment and war costs for Operations Desert Shield and Desert Storm, which are being represented by a supplemental appropriation request of $15 billion (net of allied pledges of $54.5 billion) for FY 1991.

In representing force structure, I do not count reserve units. In costing active combat forces, I take the cost of reserve forces as a kind of support cost and distribute it over the active units. Of course, the United States should have reserve (and National Guard) units for the Army, Air Force, Navy, and Marine Corps that constructively complement the active units. But, for the purposes of this study, reserve policy is not important over quite a wide range of prescriptions for organization, manning, equipment, training, and plans for emergency mobilization and deployment.

compounded, or $153 billion in 1992 dollars); require 1.1 million military personnel; and provide 6 Army divisions and 2 Marine divisions, 11 Air Force tactical air wings, and 6 carriers with 5 air wings, in addition to a diad of strategic nuclear forces consisting of submarine-launched ballistic missiles and bombers with medium-range cruise missiles. These forces, based in the United States, would not be committed to overseas defense. This program would have cost, over the seven years through 1996, $1.659 trillion and would therefore have produced a further cumulative "peace dividend," beyond the $397 billion already predictable, of $305 billion, or a total peace dividend of $702 billion.

Epilogue: A Nation among Nations

Both the administration's FY 1992 defense program and my critique are post–Persian Gulf assessments. Thus, it makes sense to talk about renewing the peace dividend. But the calculus of the peace dividend is not the whole point.

There are other factors that shape a national strategy and a defense program. But the right criterion now is not the demonstrable necessity of some precisely justified defense posture against an identified and defined threat. Rather, it is appropriateness to America's situation, both its status and role in the world and its internal constraints. The thinking must be long range and large scale—in other words, truly strategic.

American history has been marked by an oscillation between two fundamental stances toward the world: adjustment and control. These have sometimes been interpreted, tendentiously, as isolation or engagement. But national security can be found not only in the stance of control, engagement, intervention, shared risk, and containment (of whatever array of "threats"). It has been sometimes sought, and sometimes found, in the contrasting stance of adjustment, disengagement, nonintervention, even isolation, and accommodation of a plural and ultimately unmanageable world.

The American "victory" in the cold war, which consisted of outlasting the Soviet Union long enough to expose the falsities at its foundation (a somewhat different formulation from that of George Kennan), is not exploitable in terms of the ability to dominate the post–cold war order. What that 45-year struggle proved is that neither superpower could so dominate. And that will be even more the case in the future, when the international system will be more populated with autonomous powers and more fragmented among and within regions.

The episode of the Persian Gulf will be seen to prove this larger point. So "after Iraq," American foreign and military policy will have to envisage and confront a different world. And the United

States will be challenged to construct an appropriate national strategy and the defense posture and budget to implement it.

In the emerging era of international relations, even great nations—even the "sole surviving superpower," if one insists on that—will do better to adjust to the conditions of the international system than to perpetuate attempts, however attractive and apparently constructive, to control the course of events in the world. What I am proposing is a military program, a force structure, and a defense budget that are appropriate to the United States as a nation among nations in a postimperial age.

About the Author

Earl C. Ravenal, a former official in the Office of the Secretary of Defense, is Distinguished Research Professor of International Affairs at the Georgetown University School of Foreign Service and a senior fellow of the Cato Institute.

Cato Institute

Founded in 1977, the Cato Institute is a public policy research foundation dedicated to broadening the parameters of policy debate to allow consideration of more options that are consistent with the traditional American principles of limited government, individual liberty, and peace. To that end, the Institute strives to achieve greater involvement of the intelligent, concerned lay public in questions of policy and the proper role of government.

The Institute is named for *Cato's Letters*, libertarian pamphlets that were widely read in the American Colonies in the early 18th century and played a major role in laying the philosophical foundation for the American Revolution.

Despite the achievement of the nation's Founders, today virtually no aspect of life is free from government encroachment. A pervasive intolerance for individual rights is shown by government's arbitrary intrusions into private economic transactions and its disregard for civil liberties.

To counter that trend, the Cato Institute undertakes an extensive publications program that addresses the complete spectrum of policy issues. Books, monographs, and shorter studies are commissioned to examine the federal budget, Social Security, regulation, military spending, international trade, and myriad other issues. Major policy conferences are held throughout the year, from which papers are published thrice yearly in the *Cato Journal*. The Institute also publishes the quarterly magazine *Regulation* and produces a monthly audiotape series, "Perspectives on Policy."

In order to maintain its independence, the Cato Institute accepts no government funding. Contributions are received from foundations, corporations, and individuals, and other revenue is generated from the sale of publications. The Institute is a nonprofit, tax-exempt, educational foundation under Section 501(c)3 of the Internal Revenue Code.

CATO INSTITUTE
224 Second St., S.E.
Washington, D.C. 20003